RELATE

Build Meaningful, Trusting,

& Lasting Relationships...

God's Way

JOHN EATON

Copyright © 2025 John Eaton
All rights reserved.

No part of this publication may be reproduced, distributed, or transmitted in any form or by any means, including photocopying, recording, or other electronic or mechanical methods, without the prior written permission of the publisher, except in the case of brief quotations embodied in critical reviews and certain other noncommercial uses permitted by copyright law.

For permission requests, contact the author at:
john.eaton@irelatechurch.com

Publisher: Global Light Press
1312 Clearfork St.
Aubrey, TX

Cover design and interior layout by Chris Boyer, Authorentic^{SM}

Printed in the United States of America

ISBNs:
979-8-218-65632-4 (hardcover)
979-8-218-65633-1 (ebook)

Unless otherwise indicated, Scripture quotations are taken from various translations, including the King James Version (public domain), The Message (MSG), New International Version (NIV), Contemporary English Version (CEV), New Living Translation (NLT), New King James Version (NKJV), English Standard Version (ESV), and The Passion Translation (TPT). Used by permission where required. All rights reserved by their respective publishers.

This book is dedicated to the many people who have allowed me to walk with them through the RELATE process over the years. To my family—my wife Amy, our kids, my parents, and my late wife Angela—I say thank you. To my Relate Church family and to my late friend George and those in the marketplace where I've served as their chaplain, I'm deeply grateful for your stories and for the way you've shared your struggles and your lives with me along the way. What the enemy meant for harm, God has turned into something truly good! Seeing these principles at work in your lives—bringing peace, hope, reconciliation, and even promotion—has inspired me to make them available to everyone. God bless you!

CONTENTS

Preface i

Introduction viii

Chapter 1 - A Roadmap for Better Relationships 1

Chapter 2 - Your Brain and Threats 11

Chapter 3 - "R" Reroute Your Thinking 28

Chapter 4 - "E" Elevate Others 61

Chapter 5 - "L" List Your Threats 87

Chapter 6 - "A" Accept Your Part 109

Chapter 7 - "T" Turn From Your Sin to God 124

Chapter 8 - "E" Enlist Accountability 152

Chapter 9 - Doing Relationships God's Way 165

Chapter 10 - RELATE Changes Things 191

Conclusion 207

PREFACE

How My Journey to RELATE Began

I was driving back from Dallas after a day of chaplain work, on my way to meet a college friend for lunch. We had seen each other at conventions and other gatherings over the years, but this would be our first time sitting down to catch up. Despite my excitement, I could feel a hint of insecurity. Were we going to pull out the measuring stick and see who had been more successful since college? By the world's standards, I felt I'd come up short.

To top it off, I was driving my 16-year-old white Oldsmobile Eighty-Eight. If you know me, you know I'm a car guy—and this car? It was a humbling experience every time I got behind the wheel.

The red headliner sagged down, brushing my hair. The paint on the trunk and roof was peeling. The A/C had long since stopped working. Every stoplight was an anxious moment, waiting to see if the car would vapor-lock and leave me stranded, with angry drivers honking behind me. Every trip in that car was an exercise in humility.

So there I was—sweating in the Texas heat, dreading every stoplight, and praying as I drove. "God, why did You bring me here? What is it You want me to do or know? Did You bring me here to fail?" And then, in a way I can only describe as a branding iron searing my mind, I heard these words: *"It's not about forgiveness."*

I wiped the sweat from my forehead. "Then what is it about?" I asked. Suddenly, Scriptures about Christ dying once and for all flooded my mind (Romans 6:10; 1 Peter 3:18; Hebrews 10).

Could it be? Could it really be that simple? I had always heard preachers say our sins were paid for—past, present, and future. But in the same breath, they would urge us to ask God for forgiveness. What?

In that moment, everything changed. My mind began to race through the theology of it all, and then the big question came into focus: *If salvation isn't about forgiveness, then what is it about?*

And then I heard it: *"Relationship."*

I don't even remember the rest of the drive to the restaurant. The Scriptures began to come alive in a way they never had before. It was like I had stumbled upon a hidden treasure—the mystery of the Gospel unlocked. My old car, my insecurities, my self-doubt—all of it faded as I realized I was seeing God's Word through a new lens.

Reconciling the Revelation

But a revelation isn't valid unless it aligns with Scripture. And suddenly, I saw it everywhere. The commandments weren't just arbitrary rules—they were God teaching us how to relate to Him. *"Don't murder, because I don't like it. Don't worship other gods, because I want to be your only God."* Jesus didn't come to abolish the law but to fulfill it—with love (Matthew 5:17). He didn't discard the commandments; He transformed them into matters of the heart.

For years, I had lived under a theology that kept me in constant fear. I begged God for forgiveness all day long. But the truth was clear now: forgiveness was already settled at the cross. The real question is, *Do I love God enough to walk with Him—His way?*

My way of sinning, feeling guilty, and then asking for forgiveness had become a cycle of nothing more than asking for permission to sin again, without true repentance in love. To me, it was revolutionary!

When I arrived at the restaurant to meet my friend, all my previous thoughts and insecurities were laid aside. My mind was flooded with "new" information. Wiping sweat, stepping out of my Oldsmobile, I rushed inside eager to share my revelation.

Greeting him, I barely said hi before quickly explaining what had just happened—I downloaded everything to him. I couldn't contain it—it was that big. Unfortunately, his response was far less enthusiastic than mine. In fact, he rejected any notion that we have anything to do with salvation.

Talk about a letdown.

But I knew what I had discovered was true—and Scriptural. This wasn't about theological debates or denominational differences. This was about relationship.

Relationship Fulfills the Theological Differences

Everything changed for me that day. The commands of God were no longer chains keeping me from enjoying life; they were invitations into deeper love.

I started reading through the Bible all over again—but this time, through the lens of relationship. Up to that point, I had been in full-time ministry for 13 years. I was licensed and ordained, a Bible college graduate, and a front-row-note-taking Christian most of my life—and I was still asking God for forgiveness nearly every other moment of every day. Why? Because my faith was fear-driven.

For the first time, I understood what Jesus meant when He said that if we don't forgive others, our sins won't be forgiven. *If we're all forgiven once and for all, then why would Jesus say that? Isn't that a contradiction?*

Not when you consider what He was getting at—relationship. What Jesus was saying is that God isn't obligated to let us into heaven simply because we're forgiven. He's not bound by a contract. What Jesus did on the cross was make it completely and totally relational.

Perhaps this is what Jesus meant when He said He came to fulfill the law (Matthew 5:17). I call it the "Relationship Gospel." And maybe—just maybe—with this relationship gospel, the true mystery of the Gospel has been revealed.

And John wrote, *"Whoever claims to love God yet hates a brother or sister is a liar"* (1 John 4:20).

Jesus fulfilled the entirety of God's laws with just two commands: *Love God. Love people* (Matthew 22:36–40).

That is relationship.

The way we treat people is a direct reflection of how we treat God.

Jesus said:

> *"A new command I give you: Love one another. As I have loved you, so you must love one another. By this everyone will know that you are my disciples, if you love one another."* – John 13:34–35 NIV

Our love for Jesus is made known in our love for others! In Matthew chapter 25, Jesus says that if we do something as simple as give someone a cup of water in His name, we've done it directly for Him.

How we relate to people is how we relate to God.

RELATE is the path forward. It is how. It is the way back to what God has always wanted…relationship.

INTRODUCTION

"You're headed for a train wreck. Call me when it happens."

That was how I ended a premarital counseling session with a couple I had been meeting with from my church. Not exactly the most encouraging bit of advice I've ever given, but it was an honest observation.

Wouldn't you know it, just a few weeks after their wedding, I received the call. It was a mammoth train wreck. I'm talking about the kind of derailing with proverbial train cars smashed to bits and upside down in the river. The husband was doing things that threatened his new bride and their relationship, and as a result, she was totally broken.

In my thirty-plus years as a pastor and chaplain, I've facilitated many personal counseling sessions. I've seen countless couples suffering deep pain—often directed at each other through cutting words, stonewalling, and endless fights in which neither wins. In fact, every time one person in a conflict "wins," both lose.

Fortunately, this dear couple made the choice to fight for each other instead of against each other. They put in the hard work to deal with an incredibly difficult situation. With God's help, and by choosing daily to do the things we'll explore in this book, they are still married all these years later, with beautiful children and a restored relationship.

Their successful restoration began with just two words: "I'm wrong."

Trust me when I tell you, those are two of the most powerful words a person can speak. They are words that bring freedom.

Sadly, we are witnessing a troubling trend in today's society. People are growing more afraid of failing at relationships and are quicker to quit than to do what's needed to save them. Marriages, families, friendships, and even work relationships are at risk. As fear increases, many people avoid looking inward. Taking responsibility for their actions decreases. The result? A failure to grow personally—and a breakdown in relationships.

The very thing we desire—connection and closeness—is lost, leaving us alone and reeling from isolation.

Relationships are difficult. For a relationship to thrive, it requires work, patience, honest self-reflection, and selfless giving. When conflict arises, the temptation is to shrink back or sometimes lash out. Many people would rather give up than risk trying to know someone intimately. And why not? In today's world, it's easy to unfriend, ignore, or simply not invest in someone. The online world makes it easier than ever. We can pop in and out of someone's life with a simple tap or swipe.

We're seeing people make the choice to settle for digital relationships with individuals they don't even know. These relationships cost nothing and require little to no responsibility. Chatting and gaming late at night with someone in another state has become common. Some husbands and wives spend hours online with "friends" while their spouse sits in the next room. And it's even more troubling than that—our kids are growing up in a world that's replacing real relationships with virtual ones, and sometimes even non-human relationships.

AI—Artificial Intimacy

For decades, software developers and researchers have been building large language models (LLMs), a form of artificial intelligence (AI) designed to mimic human thinking and communication. What's fascinating—and alarming—is that these LLMs are capable of unsupervised training. That means the software "teaches" itself by analyzing billions of data points about how human beings communicate by monitoring our online activity. They have learned what humans value, what we desire, and what we'll do almost anything for.

These AI models can carry on conversations that are often indistinguishable from an actual person. They understand how to say exactly what the person on the other end wants to hear—except better, or worse, depending on how you view it. AI hasn't learned from watching how God thinks and communicates. It's learned from us—a humanity that, without God, always serves itself.

Imagine a relationship that's impossible to mess up. No risk of rejection. No chance of being ghosted, abandoned, or hurt. The other "person" is there no matter what you say or do. They never find you offensive or unattractive. They never push back when you're selfish. No messy emotions to deal with. In fact, they don't even have inconvenient feelings you have to deal with. The "relationship" is simply all about you.

Moreover, this "friend" seems to understand all your interests, has answers for every question, and is available day or night. They're designed to meet all your emotional needs—exactly the way *you* want them to.

Oh, how the temptation to find such a relationship can pull us in. The perfect friend. One that doesn't require love. A friend that is only there for you, at your beck and call. A friendship that doesn't require love. One that exists solely for your benefit.

But here's the truth: There is no such person.

No one exists only to meet your needs—just as you'll never

be that for anyone else. God doesn't even present Himself that way. Why? Because true relationships are a two-way road. Loving selflessly and surrendering selfish desires is required. Learning and practicing the way of love is the only path to lasting, fulfilling relationships.

That's what RELATE helps us do.

The Threat Program

Our brains are really good at perceiving danger. And our sinful hearts are wired to search *only* for what is good for *us*.

When we are confronted or feel accused, a subconscious program in our brain immediately kicks into gear. It's a defense mechanism that causes our brains to shift into self-protection mode.

For example, when someone says, "I don't appreciate what you said," or "What you did was hurtful," my brain perceives a threat and the subconscious program instantly interprets it as: *I'm just being misunderstood* or *I'm not the problem—they are.*

If someone I've hurt sets a boundary to protect themselves

from my hurtful words or actions, I might label them judgmental or overly sensitive. If this happens too many times, that person may begin to feel emotionally unsafe around me.

But what if we could have close, meaningful, long-term relationships without constantly feeling threatened when someone expresses their feelings or needs? What if we knew how to love the people in our lives in ways that helped them feel loved—without defaulting to self-protection?

Sounds amazing, doesn't it?

The good news is, it is possible—and it is God's plan for you and me.

One of the first keys to having strong relationships with both God and people is this: Learn how, and why, you're wrong.

It's important to understand—it's not necessary to always be right so that others can love you. But it *is* necessary to recognize when you're wrong—for others to feel safe relating to you.

The fight to be right is almost always wrong.

It's unhealthy—and sometimes dangerous—to be in a relationship with someone who cannot see their sin, acknowledge their wrong motives, or choose to change destructive behavior. But even with our human tendencies to prioritize self, there is a path to *being made right*—and that path is Jesus.

One of the most liberating things the Apostle Paul ever wrote was:

> *"Something has gone wrong deep within me and gets the better of me..." – Romans 7:20 MSG*

Paul knew the condition of his heart and owned it. That's one of the characteristics that qualified him to be used so greatly by God.

To see to it that Paul stayed humble, God left him with "a thorn in the flesh... a messenger of Satan" (2 Corinthians 12:7), something Paul would contend with for the rest of his life. And yet, God promised that His grace would be sufficient for Paul—just as it is for us.

If you've ever asked yourself, *What's wrong with me?*—

you're in good company. It's a great question. And the answer is: you're human. But the solution to better relationships is closer than you think.

You can be happily married.

You can have great relationships and succeed at work.

You can become the kind of person others want to be around.

You don't have to go through the rest of your life stuck—wondering why relationships keep failing or people keep leaving.

All Things Are Possible

Years ago, I was leading a small group. Across the table sat Dan, a brilliant and successful businessman. As the discussion continued, Dan slowly lowered his head and shook it in disbelief. With emotion, he said, "Wow...I've been divorced for 13 years, and all this time I thought it was her fault. It was me. I was wrong."

Dan was staggered by the realization that what he was angry

about for so many years wasn't even true. For the first time, he was seeing the truth. The truth about himself. He began to feel free. As he sat there, he also felt enormous relief from the weight he had carried for so long.

By facing his own failure, Dan began to let go of the baggage from his divorce. He realized he didn't have to stay hurt. Even more, he was free to go make things right with his ex-wife. He could make peace with her, even though they had both already moved on with new marriages. Letting go of his anger meant he could now be a better husband to his second wife. Dan understood and took responsibility for the part he played in the conflict from his first marriage. When he finally admitted to himself, he was wrong, rather than blaming someone else, Dan found freedom.

Make It Your Priority

I trust you're reading this book because you want to have healthy relationships. You want to feel closer to God and to the people in your life. Maybe you need to revisit the past so you can find healing for the sake of new or current relationships.

Christian author and speaker Lysa TerKeurst calls this "collecting, connecting, and correcting the dots." You collect what you know about yourself and past situations. Then you connect the dots for deeper understanding. As you heal, you learn to correct the dots.

This is a process you must build into your life every day. It's hard work—but the result is way more than worth it.

RELATE is a framework for building a stronger marriage, deeper friendships, and even professional growth. If you do the work and follow the process, you can heal from past pain and start building better relationships, now and moving forward.

My Challenge to You

I am challenging you to make a choice right now to do what it takes to build and keep better relationships. Make it your priority. It is certainly something God cares deeply about.

One of Jesus' priorities was relationships. He taught that when you come to worship and offer your gift to God, if you remember someone you've hurt, you must stop. Drop what you're doing, go to that person, and make it right. Then come back and worship (Matthew 5:24).

Jesus is saying: Right relationships are *that* important.

More than achievements. More than talent, wealth, or even worship itself.

As you begin RELATE, ask yourself these questions:

- Will I choose intimacy with God?
- Will I make genuine relationships with others a priority in my life?

Before we get to the next chapter, reflect on what Jesus taught about the one commandment that sums up all the rest:

> *"These words I speak to you are not incidental additions to your life, homeowner improvements to your standard of living. They are foundational words, words to build a life on. If you work these words into your life, you are like a smart carpenter who built his house on solid rock." – Matthew 7:21–25 MSG*

Love God and love people. That's the will of God.

<< QUESTIONS TO REFLECT ON >>

- Can you think of a situation that caught you off guard and changed the course of your day—or even your life?

- What would you do differently if you could do it over?

In Chapter 1, we'll look at the six-step RELATE framework, designed to supercharge your personal and spiritual growth by finding and dealing with the root causes of relational and spiritual problems.

Let's get started.

CHAPTER 1

A Roadmap for Better Relationships

Before embarking on any journey, it's essential to have a clear map to guide you. Understanding where you're headed and why each step matters will help you connect more deeply with the process. Think of this chapter as your guide to the key concepts and steps that will transform the way you approach relationships—both with God and others. Buckle up and get ready to RELATE.

"R" Stands for Reroute My Thinking

In the first step, you'll learn how your brain functions under threat—including emotional and mental threats—and why you react the way you do. Understanding these patterns is the foundation for creating healthier, stronger relationships. When we train our minds to respond to life God's way, we experience trust, emotional safety, and deeper connection with others.

Developing godly thought patterns takes work—and too often, it's work left undone. Many Christians overlook the importance of renewing their minds, which is why we see broken relationships, divided families, higher divorce rates, and toxic workplaces. Unresolved hurt, offense, and misunderstanding are often the reasons why kids grow up and want nothing to do with God or the church.

Romans 12:2 reminds us, "Do not conform to the pattern of this world, but be transformed by the renewing of your mind. Then you will be able to test and approve what God's will is—his good, pleasing and perfect will."

It is God's will for us to have healthy relationships, forgive others, and, if possible, live at peace with everyone.

The challenge is learning to recognize when you feel threatened and resist reacting with the first words or emotions that come to mind. Instead, you can learn to pause and invite God into the story unfolding in your mind. This will help you reroute your thinking so you can respond in love—and perhaps write a new story that leads to a much happier outcome.

"E" Stands for Elevate Others

This step challenges you to shift your focus outward. Elevating others is a conscious decision to adopt a servant-hearted approach and put others first in a positive way. True value is found in loving and serving the people around us—not just ourselves. One of the most significant contributions we can make to the world is the care, honor, and service we extend to others, not out of self-promotion or selfish gain.

Jesus said, "Whatever you do for others, you are doing for me" (Matthew 25). His life serves as the ultimate example of what it means to elevate others. He never used people for His own gain or harmed others to protect Himself. Even when He spoke the truth in love—challenging both His critics and His disciples—He did so with compassion and integrity.

However, elevating others doesn't mean neglecting yourself. Self-care is essential because it enables you to better serve those around you. Think of the preflight instructions on an airplane: in an emergency, you must secure your own oxygen mask before assisting others. The same principle applies to relationships—self-care isn't selfish; it's necessary. Taking care of yourself allows you to care for others more effectively.

You'll also learn how to navigate relationships with people who engage in destructive behaviors, helping you maintain healthy boundaries without compromising your values.

"L" Stands for List My Threats

In this step, we'll focus on identifying your threats and understanding their origins—an essential part of relational growth. The 12-step program of Alcoholics Anonymous incorporates a similar practice of taking inventory. It's a time-tested approach that has helped countless individuals uncover and address the root causes of their struggles.

This step isn't about introducing something new—it's about applying a proven method to gain clarity and insight into your relationships.

Recognizing and listing your perceived threats—whether related to security, social status, or intimacy—gives you the ability to confront them head-on. Rather than trying to change others or control their actions, you'll shift your focus inward and ask, "How am I being threatened?" Identifying these fears provides a starting point for your journey back to peace and stability.

Your threats can also reveal areas where your trust in God needs to grow. Like finding a hole in a tire, pinpointing these vulnerabilities allows you to address and repair them. This step will equip you to handle threats in a way that strengthens your relationships, builds trust, and fosters respect.

"A" Stands for Accept My Part

In this step, we take ownership of our role in relational struggles. This is the "No Turning Back" point in the journey. Now that you've recognized how you've felt threatened, and where your trust in God for security, social status, or relationships was lacking, you can begin to shift your response. Rather than relying on instincts or self-preservation tactics, you can choose to seek answers from God.

Most of us are familiar with the Seven Deadly Sins—and they are deadly for a reason. These behaviors don't just damage us personally; they destroy relationships and create deep division. When we feel threatened, we often turn to these sins as coping mechanisms—to protect ourselves or to harm those we perceive as threats.

The question you must ask yourself is: What sin have I been engaging in to cope with my threats? When you can answer that, you can identify your part to accept.

In this step, we'll explore how these sins take root and how to break free from them. As you learn to respond to threats with godly thinking, you'll notice a profound shift in your relationships. The people around you—especially those you love most—will begin to experience greater trust, respect, and a deeper connection with you.

"T" Stands for Turn from My Sin to God

In this step, we focus on the power of refocusing your life on

God. Many Christians get stuck trying to stop sinning, but what Jesus offers is so much greater than simply avoiding mistakes. Instead, He shows us what to start doing differently—living in a way that reflects His love and truth.

Now that you've identified your sins and threats, it's time to seek God for real change. You now have a prayer topic that God deeply cares about—confessing your sins instead of judging others. But true repentance goes beyond words. God calls us to take action. If possible, we are to make things right with those we've wronged. Confession is important, but restoration is proof of true repentance.

> *"This is how I want you to conduct yourself in these matters. If you enter your place of worship and, about to make an offering, you suddenly remember a grudge a friend has against you, abandon your offering, leave immediately, go to this friend and make things right. Then and only then, come back and work things out with God."* – Matthew 5:23-24 MSG

Confessing sin to God isn't just about admitting wrongdoing—it's about acknowledging the deeper sin of neglecting love and choosing better actions moving forward. Every yes to sin is a no to something greater:

- Saying yes to pride is saying no to humility.

- Embracing greed is rejecting generosity.

- Choosing drunkenness means neglecting family and responsibilities.

- Giving in to lust means missing out on lasting love.

Your repentance is proven not just by what you say but by your willingness to make amends.

"E" Stands for Enlist Accountability

In this final step, we recognize that lasting change requires accountability. Secret sin wields power—but confession and accountability break the chains of isolation and imprisonment that sin so easily brings.

> *"Make this your common practice: Confess your sins to each other and pray for each other so that you*

can live together whole and healed. The prayer of a person living right with God is something powerful to be reckoned with. Elijah, for instance, human, just like us, prayed hard that it wouldn't rain, and it didn't—not a drop for three and a half years. Then he prayed that it would rain, and it did. The showers came, and everything started growing again. My dear friends, if you know people who have wandered off from God's truth, don't write them off. Go after them. Get them back and you will have rescued precious lives from destruction and prevented an epidemic of wandering away from God." – James 5:16-20 MSG

Stronger relationships are essential to living better and receiving encouragement to never give up. One of the greatest spiritual experiences is confessing one's sins to a friend—and still being loved. Receiving someone else's love after sinning shows us that accepting God's love is possible.

In this chapter, we will explore the importance of having people in our lives who challenge us when necessary. Growth doesn't happen in isolation, and surrounding ourselves only with people who agree with us can be a serious problem.

A healthy church community should provide this kind of accountability and encouragement. But it's not just about what we receive—we are also called to offer this to others. True Christian community is a safe space where people can practice love, overcome failures, learn from mistakes, and start again.

That is RELATE in a nutshell. But before we dive deeper into how your brain works when threatened and each step of RELATE, I want to share real-life examples of how this framework has transformed relationships.

<< QUESTIONS TO REFLECT ON >>

- How do you currently respond to people who challenge or criticize you? How can you view such challenges as opportunities for growth?

CHAPTER 2

Your Brain and Threats

Threats Happen at Work

The elevator doors were about to close when Cindy rushed forward and thrust her arm between them just in time. As the doors slid open, she stepped inside—and instantly realized who was standing in front of her. Not just another employee—the company president.

Going up five floors was plenty of time for a polite exchange, but he said nothing. He didn't even glance at her. Instead, he stared at his phone, his expression unreadable. The silence was suffocating.

As soon as the doors opened, Cindy bolted out, her mind

racing. Had she just annoyed the most important man in the company? Was he frustrated with her for holding up the elevator? Was she about to lose her job? She spent the rest of the day at her desk, stomach in knots, anxiously waiting for bad news.

Threats Happen on the Roadway

Bill was driving down the tollway, enjoying a smooth commute, listening to the radio, and mentally organizing his day. Then, out of nowhere, another car cut him off, forcing him to slam on his brakes. The near miss sent a jolt of adrenaline through his body, and before he even realized it, he was yelling, throwing up his hands, and letting his frustration spill out in a string of verbal and nonverbal protests.

The moment passed—but his mood didn't. The rest of his day felt like it had been hijacked.

Threats Happen on the Field

I vividly remember Super Bowl XLVIII. Peyton Manning and the Denver Broncos took on the Seattle Seahawks. But their biggest opponent that night wasn't the team across the field—it was themselves.

On the very first play of the game, the snap came early—unexpected. I can still see it in my mind's eye as Peyton, seemingly in slow motion, watched the ball sail past him into the end zone. A safety—two points for Seattle. From that moment on, the Broncos never regained their footing. One mistake set the tone for the entire game. They never recovered. The final score? A brutal 43–8 loss.

How Your Brain Works When You Are Threatened

Our days are filled with moments like these—events that catch us off guard, moments we wish we could do over, situations where we feel like we've lost control and desperately want to take it back.

Our brains are wired to protect us. When something happens—when we feel embarrassed, insulted, threatened, or slighted—our minds immediately jump to conclusions to explain the situation. And often, the first conclusion we land on is the worst one.

Cindy assumed the president was upset with her. But what if she had written a different story in her mind? Maybe he was reading a difficult text about a family emergency. Maybe he was preparing for a tough investor meeting. Maybe he simply wasn't the type to make small talk in an elevator.

Bill believed the driver who cut him off thought he was better than him—that it was personal. But what if Bill had considered another possibility? Maybe the driver was rushing to the hospital. Maybe he'd made an honest mistake. Maybe he wasn't thinking clearly—just like Bill himself had done before.

And what if Peyton Manning and the Broncos had been able to mentally reset after that bad snap? What if, instead of allowing one mistake to define them, they had shaken it off and focused on the next play? They were the favored team. They probably could have won.

Many writers have explored this topic, but one of my favorites is David Rock, author of *Your Brain at Work*. Rock explains how we think and make decisions—especially in moments of perceived threat.

CHAPTER 2 - YOUR BRAIN AND THREATS

Your Threat Detector, Thinking Spot, and Vault

At the center of the brain is the limbic system, a complex network that is constantly scanning for threats. It's always calculating, measuring the possibility of harm, and alerting the rest of the brain when it detects danger.

For example, if your phone lights up and you see the name of someone you owe money to, your limbic system reacts. If the chair you're sitting in suddenly shifts, it sends an alert. Without your limbic system, you wouldn't survive long—because you wouldn't recognize threats until it was too late.

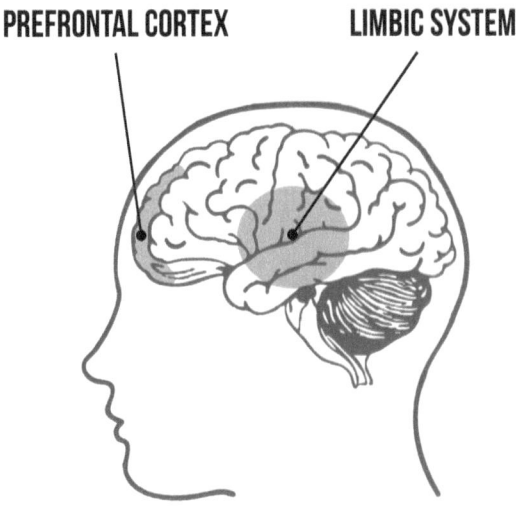

Now, let's move to another part of the brain—your thinking spot. At the very front, behind your forehead, is the prefrontal cortex—the center of conscious, intentional thought. This is where reasoning, decision-making, and self-control happen. It's what separates you from animals. It's where you make choices.

Have you ever driven home and realized you don't remember the drive? You navigated stop signs, traffic lights, and turns without even thinking about it. That's because the back part of your brain stored those learned patterns, allowing you to drive on autopilot. Your prefrontal cortex wasn't engaged because no new, complex decisions were needed.

In the back of your brain is a vast storage area—your vault. It contains your memories, your values, and your natural reactions in life.

- Memories come from your life experiences, learning, and past choices.

- Values are formed by your upbringing, spiritual guidance, and personal convictions.

- Natural responses are the ways you've always reacted—especially in times of threat.

Every conscious decision you make requires you to engage your vault—pulling information from past experiences, values, and learned reactions.

Thinking Takes Effort

Conscious thinking—the kind that requires focus, awareness, and decision-making—happens in the prefrontal cortex. It's work.

For example, if someone invites you to lunch, your prefrontal cortex immediately starts pulling information from your vault:

Do I have an appointment?
What does this invitation mean?
What will others think?
Do I even like this person?
Am I usually successful in social situations?

In a split second, your brain scans your experiences, values, and current schedule to determine your response. It's work—

and work can feel like a threat.

The Threat Response and Brain Shrinkage

Here's the problem—and I want you to let this sink in:

When the limbic system detects a threat, your prefrontal cortex physically shrinks. It limits your ability to think clearly, reason well, and access your memories and values in that moment.

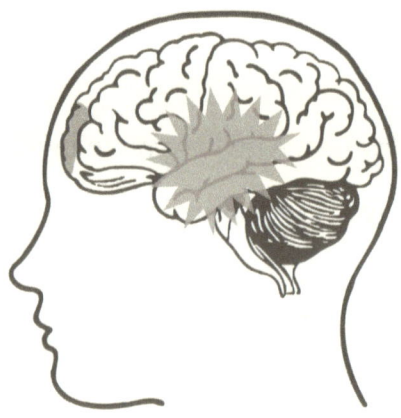

The limbic system sends out a "threat alert," and the prefrontal cortex shrinks in proportion to the perceived danger.

So, let's go back to that lunch invitation. Imagine you're at your desk, and someone walks up and asks, "Want to do lunch today?" Just as they do, your phone lights up with a message from your boss. If your boss is a source of anxiety, your limbic system reacts—sending out threat chemicals.

Suddenly, your prefrontal cortex shrinks. Even answering a simple question feels overwhelming. In that moment, you'll default to your most natural response—whatever you've always done in times of threat.

Or imagine you're on the highway and someone slams on their brakes in front of you. You react immediately—hitting your brakes and avoiding a crash. The actual danger? A fender bender. But now your brain starts running scenarios:

Did they do that on purpose?
Are they mad at me?
Do they think they're better than me?

Suddenly, it's not about safety anymore—it's personal. And your natural response takes over, escalating the situation unnecessarily.

The greater the threat your brain perceives, the more your prefrontal cortex shrinks—and the less control you have over how you respond.

Memories and Values Take a Back Seat to Natural Responses

Let me restate what happens:

When your brain detects a threat, your prefrontal cortex shrinks. Your ability to think clearly and make wise decisions is limited. Your vault—full of memories, values, and learned experiences—is available to help you, but without serious effort and practice, you'll default to your natural responses.

Your natural responses have well-worn, high-speed highways leading to them. Your memories and values? They have tiny footpaths. Unless you've intentionally trained your mind to access them, they'll go untapped when the pressure hits—and you'll default to instinct.

Ever walked up to a keypad and forgotten the code you've used for years? Or blanked on your debit card PIN? Something threatened you—a word, a smell, a sound—and your brain defaulted to survival mode, cutting off access to what you already know.

The military trains soldiers to overcome this. They call it *battle-proofing* or *battle inoculation*. Through repetitive drills, soldiers learn to access their values and training under pressure. First responders do the same. They condition themselves to move toward danger when others run away. They don't have to think—they've trained their minds to choose the right response.

Humans Are Different—We Can Reflect

Humans have the unique ability to reflect on our behavior—to step back and view ourselves like an outside observer. Social neuroscience still can't fully explain why. Unlike animals, we can choose to change our course.

Think of it like this:

Your thoughts are like water. Over time, they carve grooves—paths your mind automatically follows.

Sometimes, those grooves lead to joyful memories. Other times, they send you spiraling into fear, insecurity, or dread.

These default paths aren't just about memories—they shape how you see the future too. In times of threat, you will automatically follow those familiar paths unless you train yourself to reroute.

The Role of the Director

David Rock refers to this conscious decision-maker as *the director*. It's the part of you that takes note of what's happening and chooses how to respond.

But your brain also has a *default map*—those preprogrammed pathways formed by past experiences and emotions.

This is where the director must step in. Without intervention, your brain runs on autopilot, reacting from old patterns. But with conscious effort, your director can override the default and lead you to a different response.

When conflict arises—say, an argument with your spouse—you have a choice:

CHAPTER 2 - YOUR BRAIN AND THREATS

1. Will you let your default map take over, dragging you through years of resentment and unresolved pain?

2. Or will you engage your director, choosing to respond in a way that reflects the future you want for your marriage?

But be aware—you have only a small window, one or two seconds, to activate the director before your limbic system hijacks your response. When the prefrontal cortex shrinks, your natural response takes over: fight, flight, freeze, or faint.

So let me ask:

How well has your instinctive reaction worked for you?

Are your fights productive—or do they leave people exhausted and hurt?

Do you avoid conflict entirely, hoping problems will fix themselves?

Are you drained from trying to prove you belong and are accepted?

Move from Fear to Courage

Courage is a choice. It comes from within. It's your director speaking truth to you—and you choosing to listen.

For every fear, there's a step of courage waiting. God wants to teach you how. That's what the RELATE process will help you do.

How old will you be before you are free from what happened to you as a child?

How many decades will pass before you stop punishing yourself for teenage mistakes?

How long will your spouse have to pay for the failures of your parents—or the sins of your ex?

It's time to fight. Time to take courage. Time to move onto the battlefield and defeat fear.

A Story of Courage

General George S. Patton was a man of extraordinary bravery. Known for his relentless pursuit of victory, he refused to let fear dictate his mission. But what made him remarkable wasn't just what he said—it was how he lived.

One of my favorite untold stories about Patton came from a chaplain friend whose father, Buck Sergeant, Ron Bartoo, served under General Patton's command in France during World War II.

One day, Patton approached Bartoo and ordered, "Go get that Jeep. You're going to be my driver today."

Without hesitation, Bartoo obeyed. As they drove, Patton directed him toward a ridge deep in enemy territory. Bartoo and another officer grew increasingly nervous, knowing they were driving straight into danger.

When the officer finally spoke up, Patton barked, "Keep going!"

They parked the Jeep, and Patton ordered them to follow him on foot—fully exposed to enemy fire. Mortar shells fell around them, each one closer than the last. Every time, Bartoo and the officer dove to the ground. But Patton? He simply turned his back to the blast, shielding his front side, and kept moving. When they reached the vantage point, Patton raised his binoculars, surveyed the enemy's position, and calmly said, "That's it, fellas. Let's get out of here."

Bartoo later told his son, "I've never seen anyone without fear like that man."

But was Patton truly fearless?

One of his lesser-known quotes says otherwise:

"If we take the generally accepted definition of bravery as a quality which knows no fear, I have never seen a brave man. All men are frightened. The more intelligent they are, the more they are frightened."

Patton wasn't reckless—he had learned how to master his mind. He rerouted his thinking. He engaged his director. That's what made him courageous.

And you can too.

CHAPTER 2 - YOUR BRAIN AND THREATS

<< QUESTIONS TO REFLECT ON >>

- When you feel threatened, what is your natural response? Anger? Avoidance? Numbing?

- Are there values you hold that you consistently violate in moments of stress?

- How often is fear driving your behavior, rather than faith or purpose?

- What default responses in moments of threat are damaging your relationships?

CHAPTER 3

"R" Reroute Your Thinking

Now that you understand more about how your brain becomes restrained when you are threatened, let's move to the first step in RELATE. Rerouting Your Thinking is what you do whenever you experience an emotional derailment—whether big or small—you take control and change its course.

Rerouting your thinking isn't just about improving your mood; it means pausing and considering the possibility of another story, so that you can *respond,* not just *react.* When you recognize that your first reaction isn't always the best one, you can step back, reframe the situation, and take control of your response. That small shift can save relationships, protect your peace, and even set you up for success in ways you never imagined. Jeremiah wrote, *"The heart is deceitful above all things, and desperately wicked: who can know it?" (Jer. 17:9 KJV)*.

In other words, every experience you have is filtered through a heart that is naturally flawed—a heart that deceives even you. Your heart's primary instinct is self-preservation, which means it will often misinterpret situations in an attempt to protect you.

Until you take the time to examine your intentions and emotions—to understand what's really driving you—you will struggle to fully love God and those around you. You may find that people keep their distance, that relationships feel strained, or that others seem guarded around you. Why? Because it's hard for them to trust someone who trusts their own corrupt heart.

Rerouting your thinking creates space for people to feel safe with you. It allows them to trust you, open up, and build deeper connections.

The threats you perceive in life often stem from a place of

self-preservation. Your brain, influenced by a heart that is naturally deceitful, may convince you that danger is present when, in reality, the threat isn't real. Rerouting your thinking gives you the time and perspective to investigate those threats—to pause and discern whether you are truly at risk or whether fear is simply leading you astray. It is a conscious, intentional choice to refuse to let fear dictate your life.

Rerouting Fear into Courage

A great benefit of reading Bible stories and God's interaction with us is to see how He has taught us to do these very things. But more than that, as His followers, He expects us to trust Him and not let fear keep us from carrying out His meaningful plan.

How big of a deal would it have been if the people involved in Jesus's life had let fear stop them? When Joseph was afraid to take Mary as his wife, the angel came and spoke to him—becoming his director, feeding him truth. The first thing he told him was "Do not be afraid" (Matthew 1:20). Then he accessed his memories. He reminded him of his faith—that the Messiah would come and save us (Matthew 1:21).

In other words, *these are your values. Remember what you have been taught about this. This is what you believe. Now it's happening, and you need to take courage and not abandon Mary!*

Around the same time, something similar happened with Zechariah, John the Baptist's father. Gabriel came to him and the first thing he said was, *"Do not be afraid..."* (Luke 1:13). He told him he would have a son, just as he had prayed. Then he gave him instructions on how to raise him and told him how this son would be used mightily to announce to the world that the Messiah is here. Gabriel was directing him, speaking truth. He then accessed Zechariah's memories, reminding him of the Messiah his parents had taught him about and pointing him back to his faith. But Zechariah didn't believe him. He didn't let the director reroute his thinking. So, God muted him until months later when the boy was born, and Zechariah named him John—finally obeying the director. Suddenly, he could speak again.

Imagine how many people—and God—were counting on these two men to lay aside their fear and take courage. God was so adamant that Zechariah stay faithful that He muted him. A lot was riding on this being done. You need to know that God has purpose and meaning for your life. So long as you live in fear, His will and the very reason you are alive gets muted. God wants you to rise above fear and live courageously.

Perhaps you've heard the phrase "fight or flight." But your brain doesn't just fight or flee—it can also freeze or faint. Since the Fall of Man in Genesis, human brains have defaulted to self-preservation mode, reacting instinctively to anything perceived as a threat. As we learned in the previous chapter, this response is chemical and automatic.

The frustrating part? Most of the time, this defense mechanism isn't necessary. Unfortunately, that means we often react to situations that were never a real danger in the first place. The only threat was the one we imagined.

The problem is that our threats are filtered through a corrupt, self-centered, and self-preserving brain and heart. We excuse bad behavior because of this and sometimes even rationalize negative attitudes and unhealthy choices.

You may have heard that the acronym for fear is F.E.A.R.: False Evidence Appearing Real. It describes how our minds can create a false story about how a situation will turn out.

F.E.A.R. keeps you focused only on immediate threats, blinding you from seeing long-term consequences.

If a honeybee flies into your car, what's the worst it can do? Sting you once. That's it. But the normal human reaction is chaos—flailing arms, screaming, total panic. If you lose control like that, what's the worst that could happen? Definitely more than a sting.

This all comes back to using the director I introduced in the previous chapter—using your real self to make decisions. Left on autopilot, without intentional, God-focused thinking, your fear can destroy both your peace and your relationships.

What you think is most important at this moment may not be.

What you believe is an actual threat today may not be. You

might have made it up to ease your own fear.

What you believe someone is thinking about you is often not the case.

What you are afraid of will likely never happen.

What you are running from probably isn't even chasing you.

Remember, your brain's job is to protect you, so it constantly scans for threats. But if it can't find one, that's a problem—because not knowing what the threat is becomes a threat. Often, when no obvious danger exists, your brain will fabricate one just to feel more secure.

For instance, people with a lot of money sometimes lose their minds trying to find a challenge in life. Wives with easygoing husbands who never get upset tell me, "I wish my husband would fight with me about something!" Their brain needs to know the current threat, and if there isn't one, that's a threat.

Rerouting your thinking is a decision to take on a default attitude of courage. Instead of immediately letting fear grip you and overtake your thoughts and reactions, you apply courage to every situation and look for other interpretations that are more aligned with reality.

Just Forgive or Find Truth

Rerouting your thinking will often move in one of two directions—and sometimes both. One, simply forgive. Or two, seek truth.

Sometimes your immediate response to a threat can be to pause and say, "Okay God, I'm not sure what that was about, but I give it to You and let it go." You trust God with what was said or done. A good indicator that this was the right move is that you don't walk away feeling like a victim. You walk away free and without emotional baggage.

But when you can't just forgive and release it, you need to pursue truth. What was really said? What did they actually mean? What really happened? Investigate to see if the story your heart told your brain was accurate. Most of the time, it wasn't the whole story. Often, it's a misunderstanding or misinterpretation. And once you get clarity, you can walk away with peace—and the relationship can even grow stronger as a result.

You'll discover that you need both the truth and trust in God to really forgive others.

Rerouting Frustration Into Faith

I recently spoke with a teacher who had been using the RELATE process and shared how it helped her rediscover her love for teaching. She had always respected her position and valued the opportunity to shape young minds. But over time, the reality of the job—the daily challenges and difficult students—had drained her passion. She was exhausted.

Each day felt like a battle. She found herself resenting students who didn't seem to care about learning and growing bitter toward parents who, in her eyes, didn't enforce discipline or respect. She began dreading going to work and even started considering a career change.

One day, she decided to sit down, pray, and walk through the RELATE process. As she rerouted her thinking, she saw something she hadn't seen before—she was called to serve these kids. Not just as their teacher, but as someone who could intercede for them.

CHAPTER 3 - REROUTE YOUR THINKING

"They need someone to silently pray over them," she realized.

"They need someone to see past who they are right now and believe in who they can become."

In this case, she found truth—and she chose to forgive.

By recognizing her own selfishness and lack of trust in God, she experienced a complete transformation. She began going to work with peace and joy—not because her students suddenly changed, or because she received a heartfelt letter of gratitude from a former student, or because a parent finally thanked her. Things changed because she changed.

She rerouted her thinking.

Like General Patton, from the previous chapter, she stepped onto the battlefield of her daily life with a new perspective—ready to fight for something greater than herself.

Mirror, Mirror...

One of the biggest mistakes we make is assuming that what we think and feel is reality—or even worse, that it's absolute truth. We also tend to believe that others should instinctively know what we're thinking and feeling, and we expect them to respond accordingly.

Consider this: You're on vacation and approach a local for help, only to be met with an eye roll or a sigh because your question seems obvious to them. But what's common knowledge to them isn't common knowledge to you. We often assume that what we know is just common sense, but in reality, people aren't privy to what's in our minds. To get upset with others for not understanding our thoughts or feelings is a mistake—one that needs to be taken through RELATE.

In August 2017, my home was struck by lightning while my family was away on vacation. We had prayed as we left, never imagining we wouldn't have a home to return to. After coming back to the aftermath, I was driving one day when someone cut me off. That simple act triggered a flood of emotions—anger, frustration, and a deep sense of injustice. My brain told me I deserved to be treated differently because of my suffering. And beyond that, I felt like everyone around me somehow knew, or *should* have known, what I was going through and should act accordingly. Looking back, I can see how irrational that was. But in the moment, it felt real.

Years later, when my wife passed away, I recognized those same feelings creeping in again—but this time, I knew how to handle them.

The reality is people aren't thinking about us nearly as much as we assume they are.

My son learned this lesson when he had a giant zit on his nose for two weeks. He has a great sense of humor but wasn't thrilled about looking like Rudolph the Red Nosed Reindeer at work; especially around the girls. On the way to drop him off, I told him, "Nobody's paying attention to it. And if they do notice, they're probably just relieved it's not happening to them." He laughed, but I could see the relief in his eyes. That small shift in perspective allowed him to move on.

It's as if we live behind a one-way mirror. As we look around, we see everyone else, and we think they're looking back at us. In reality, they're seeing their own reflection.

I experienced this firsthand when I had skin cancer on my nose. After surgery, I wore bright white bandages for weeks while making corporate chaplain visits. When the bandages came off, the scars were obvious for months. I assumed everyone I interacted with would remember seeing me like that.

But a year later, when I mentioned it in conversation, people looked confused.

"When did that happen?"

"Did I see you during that time?"

"I don't remember that at all."

It was a humbling realization: something that had felt so significant to me had barely registered with anyone else.

This awareness is a powerful tool in rerouting our thinking. We naturally evaluate ourselves in every interaction, filtering conversations through how they affect *us*. When someone shares good news, we wonder why it didn't happen to us. When someone shares a hardship, we immediately relate it to what would happen if *we* were in their shoes.

CHAPTER 3 - REROUTE YOUR THINKING

If you tell a coworker you were reprimanded by the boss, they're not thinking about how difficult it must have been for you. They're wondering if they're next. If you mention a loved one has passed away, their mind jumps to when they lost someone, or what it will be like when they lose someone dear to them.

Understanding this doesn't mean people are selfish—it means they're human. And knowing this truth is a great help in rerouting your thinking, freeing you from the false assumption that everyone is focused on you.

Without the mental and emotional conditioning that comes from spiritual maturity, most people remain stuck at this lower level of relationships. RELATE moves you beyond instinct.

More Than Animals

While visiting Juneau, Alaska, I wandered to the edge of town, taking in the scenery. A creek ran from the seaport, flowing under the road and toward the base of the mountain. As I stopped on a bridge to look down, I saw the salmon running.

RELATE

Watching them struggle was a strange mix of awe and sadness. They fought against the current, pushing forward with everything they had. But then I looked ahead. A couple hundred yards upstream, the creek turned into a giant concrete culvert—flat, shallow, with barely half an inch of water running off the mountain. And there, scattered along the culvert, were fish flopping helplessly. They had followed their instincts, but it had led them nowhere. Their journey, meant for spawning and new life, had hit a dead end.

It seemed right. It felt like they were following their created purpose. But instinct alone had failed them.

God gave humans something greater than instinct—the ability to think beyond it.

If we only followed our most basic impulses, we'd live like those salmon, mindlessly pursuing what feels right, never realizing we're headed for a dead end. Instinct might tell us to chase pleasure, satisfy every desire, put ourselves first, and survive at all costs. But God has given us the ability to see farther than our instincts allow.

This is what I call *animalistic relatability*—the most basic, shallow, instinct-driven way to exist. And in today's world, technology makes it easier than ever to live at this level.

We no longer need deep relationships to survive. Unlike past generations, we don't have to know the butcher, the blacksmith, the cobbler, or even the banker. Everything we need is just a click away. We can order groceries, get a loan, and even form relationships—all without ever seeing another human face-to-face.

Technology has made it possible to have just enough connection to keep us going, but not enough to make us truly known. We can even find false intimacy online, never having to meet in person. No effort. No accountability. No real risk.

We don't have to get dressed to shop. We don't even have to shower to go on a "date." It can all happen right there in the comfort of our living room—alone. Everyone for themselves.

But is that really living?

Any sudden movement threatens a cat. Its body tenses, eyes

sharpen with focus, and it reacts instinctively. A dogs is territorial—if it senses its space being invaded, a dog will respond out of pure instinct. A mother bear won't pause to consider your intentions if you get too close to her cubs. She won't reason with you or give you the benefit of the doubt. She won't ask questions or listen to explanations. She will simply react.

Unlike animals, we have the privilege of language and communication to prevent these kinds of misunderstandings. More than that, we have something animals don't—a God-given moral compass. Our morals can become instinctual, guiding our decisions without us having to think about them.

Animals don't stop to consider whether their actions are morally right or wrong. They simply do what their nature dictates. But we serve a living God who has personally shown us how to rise above base, survival-driven instincts. That's what the Cross was about. Jesus didn't just tell us what it looks like to live differently—He demonstrated it. And He commands us to do the same.

Rerouting your thinking is your opportunity to tell a different story than the one your instincts immediately feed you. Instead of automatically reacting to perceived threats, you can stop, step back, and choose to believe a different version of events. Without this discipline, you are left at the mercy of your animalistic impulses—and they will ruin relationships, destroy opportunities, and lead you in the wrong direction. Because the first story you tell yourself isn't always the truth. And we make life-altering decisions based on those false narratives all the time.

God granted mankind dominion over the earth (Genesis 1:28-31). He called us to use it, create from it, sustain ourselves with it, and manage it. When the world faced destruction, it wasn't the animals that built the ark—it was Noah and his family. And Jesus made it clear:

> *"You are worth much more than many sparrows."*
> – Luke 12:7, CEV

Jesus didn't have to die for the sins of animals. They show aggression, are territorial, fight for dominance, and take what they want—but they don't need a Savior to reconcile them to

God. Humans are different. We are *relatable*. We have been given the ability to make moral decisions—not just based on instinct, but on what we know God desires.

> *"You made them a little lower than the angels; you crowned them with glory and honor and put everything under their feet. In putting everything under them, God left nothing that is not subject to them."*
> – Hebrews 2:7-8, NIV

God calls us—and all creation expects us—to live above our base instincts. Instincts tells us to protect ourselves at all costs. A mother bear will shelter her cubs fiercely, but a loving human mother will train her child to one day live a moral and godly life on their own. Animals fight to defend their territory, but a godly man or woman will use their territory to bless, shelter, and provide for others.

We are called to a higher standard of living.

Look ahead. Where is your current path leading? Is it a dead end? Are you simply working, striving, surviving—only to reach the inevitable like those salmon?

Living by instinct alone isn't enough.

A Spiritual Perspective: The Soul as the Director

Here's where it gets even more interesting for followers of Christ.

What if...your soul is the Director? What if the real you—your soul—is that voice you use to talk to your brain?

Think about it. The prefrontal cortex is the only part of your brain where:

- You have conscious, intentional thought.

- You can decide to stop thinking about one thing and start thinking about another.

- You choose which memories and values to pull from when making decisions.

When John the Baptist and Jesus preached, *"Change your life, God's Kingdom is here" (Matthew 3:2, MSG),* they were essentially saying: *Because you know God's kingdom is real, let your soul lead—direct—your brain and body!*

Your flesh feels threatened, but your soul isn't. No human can threaten or destroy your soul. Your soul will never act or react out of fear or threats. The real you is completely sane!

With God, your soul will never die, never starve, never be in danger. Let your soul win over your flesh—the part of you that craves what destroys relationships, peace, and purpose.

Let your soul begin to tell your body where to go and what to do. Let love dictate your actions and reactions. This is the answer Paul was searching for in Romans 7 when he grew exasperated with his own behavior (Romans 7:14ff). The things he knew God didn't like; he kept doing. And the things he knew God wanted him to do, he struggled to carry out consistently. He knew the goal in our spiritual walk is to stop doing what God doesn't like and start doing what He does like. It's all about loving Him—relationship.

CHAPTER 3 - REROUTE YOUR THINKING

Rerouting My Thinking Takes Practice

My daughter is a brilliant student but a terrible test-taker. She aces her homework, understands concepts, and has common sense—but when the test lands in front of her, all that knowledge locks itself in a vault. Why?

The threat of failure overwhelms her brain. The fear of being seen as less intelligent than her brother, who earned a full-ride scholarship from his ACT score, floods her system. Her memory is there—but her limbic system has triggered a threat alert, blocking access to it.

Her mother and I coached her through RELATE, helping her understand that when she feels threatened, her brain is the real barrier—not her intelligence.

Rerouting your thinking requires training and repetition. You must stop your mind from taking the easy route and intentionally redirect it to the right path. Learning to access your values and past experiences in the middle of a threat takes effort. More than that—you only have one or two seconds to do it before your prefrontal cortex shrinks.

And here's the twist: rerouting your thinking is itself a threat.

Rerouting My Thinking Takes Work

Using your conscious mind requires effort. And effort feels like a threat.

Think about driving. One of the reasons we get so angry when someone cuts us off isn't just that they're driving dangerously—it's because they force us to wake up. We were on cruise control, lost in thought, and suddenly, we have to think. We feel threatened—not by the driver, but by the work it takes to re-engage.

Thinking is a subtle threat. You don't mind answering 2+2, but if someone asks you to subtract 234 from 537 in your head, your brain resists. You could do it if you focused and concentrated—but that requires work.

Our entire culture is built around avoiding work. Every commercial promises to make life easier. Even churches try to make it easier to get to heaven. If we could, we'd just hit cruise control and drift through life to eternity. But that's not how transformation happens.

CHAPTER 3 - REROUTE YOUR THINKING

The Danger of "Cruise Control" Thinking

My late wife's lasagna was legendary. When I would sit down to start eating it, and then take a bite of warm bread, I entered into a dope-minded bliss, moving my fork from plate to mouth on autopilot, with no thinking involved whatsoever.

One night, while I was fully absorbed in what was on my plate, she interrupted my trance and asked, "Well, is anyone enjoying the meal?" I hadn't complimented her cooking.

BOOM! She cut me off. My mental cruise control was suddenly interrupted. While I was mindlessly, and literally, stuffing my face, I was threatening her. I didn't realize what I was communicating was, "You are expected to give me this, and you don't matter." While I was going to town with my fork, she was feeling taken for granted with every bite. I was completely oblivious.

In that moment, we both felt a threat. My brain thought, *Why can't I just enjoy what you made? It's my right to delight without having to think about it!* Her brain thought, *Does anyone appreciate that I put care and effort into this meal?*

She wasn't just asking for a compliment—she was seeking acknowledgment. She had worked hard on that meal. But I had unknowingly communicated, *I shouldn't have to stop and think about you.*

I didn't mean to send that message, but my lack of awareness was a threat to her. In return, her request for acknowledgment was a threat to me.

This happens in relationships all the time. One person is in their own world, unaware, and the other person feels hurt or ignored. The result? A bad night ahead.

Renewing our minds is work. And it's the work that, unfortunately, our culture seems to be avoiding. God has called us to be transformed by the renewing of our minds (Romans 12:2).

Avoiding False Alarms

Not knowing the real threats of life can leave us feeling insecure—and threatened even more.

Children need reasonable, negative feedback from their parents now and then. It reassures them of their boundaries and helps them feel more secure. The same is true in the workplace. If your boss gives you small critiques, it's a sign they're paying attention and aren't secretly worried about bigger issues.

We all know life isn't that easy. When all is well, we sense something is always "cooking" in the pressure pot, and not knowing what it is causes our brain to react. It knows this is too good to be true—it's a threat. I've seen people, both men and women, convince themselves their spouse was having an affair—without a shred of evidence, simply because their brains latched onto that fear. In the end, they destroyed the very relationship they were desperate to protect.

Employers who give consistent, honest feedback prevent this kind of paranoia in the workplace. But how do you react when your boss critiques your work? Are you grateful? Defensive? Dismissive? Do you start comparing yourself to others? When someone in authority gives you feedback, it is wise to listen, learn, and adjust. Avoiding feedback can lead to feeling insecure and limit your ability to grow.

The same principle applies in relationships. If you nitpick the feedback you get from your spouse, friend, pastor, or boss—always demanding clarification in an effort to prove your innocence—it's exhausting, for you and them.

What if, instead, you simply listened, learned, and adjusted? If they are wrong, trust that time will reveal the truth. Your restraint in making a big emotional issue out of it will gain you far more trust and respect than arguing ever could.

The best mindset for receiving negative feedback is this: They are teaching me how to keep the relationship.

Having a trusted friend outside of your immediate circle can bring clarity when your brain starts creating false threats. When in doubt, wait before reacting. Within a few days, the issue will likely prove itself to be nothing, and your relationships will be spared from unnecessary drama.

Where Wisdom Begins

Our threats divide us. Everyone has threats, and everyone believes their threat is the most important—and we get frustrated that others don't agree. So, who is right? That's the big question.

Take Christian churches, for example. We have so many diverse types of churches, worship structures, and styles—all of which are about people choosing a less threatening way to walk with God. Some need more structure and rules to feel comfortable. Others want less. Who is right?

Some churches reject certain styles of music because they believe instruments are unbiblical. Others have a full rock band with smoke machines and flashing lights.

Some have plush pews and an ornate altar, while others have stackable chairs so the kids can play basketball in the sanctuary after service. The differences seem like diversity, but more often than not, they're about people managing their perceived threats.

A man once attended my church for a couple of years. He became a good friend, but he held a strong belief that a particular Bible translation was corrupt. He said using it in our church was like "poisoning the people." After studying the issue myself,

I didn't agree with him, but I respected his conviction. To keep the peace, I told him I would refrain from using that version when he and his family were present.

That wasn't enough for him. It wasn't just about what I read; he needed me to agree with him completely. When I wouldn't, he left the church. I still think about him today. He was funny, bright, and a unique individual. I'm sad that we're no longer working together in the Kingdom, serving God.

Why do so many people draw such hard lines on issues that are inconsequential? Because we often believe God is like us, forgetting that we are called to become like Him. If it threatens me, it must be a threat to God...

> *"The fear of the Lord is the beginning of wisdom."*
> – Proverbs 9:10, NIV

Until we realize that being called to God's way is our only real "threat," everything else we think we know is unimportant.

Because, with God, we can lose everything—our wealth, our health, even loved ones—and still have hope for eternity. But without God, our only hope is to survive another day.

Reroute Your Thinking

Jesus said:

"Do not be afraid of those who kill the body but cannot kill the soul. Rather, be afraid of the One who can destroy both soul and body in hell." – Matt. 10:28, NIV

So, who is right? About everything? The obvious answer is: God is.

The Bible is filled with what God likes and doesn't like. The Ten Commandments were just the starting point. But when Jesus came, He simplified it all:

"Love the Lord your God with all your heart and with all your soul and with all your mind. This is the first and greatest commandment. And the second is like it: Love your neighbor as yourself. All the Law and the Prophets hang on these two commandments."
– Matthew 22:37-40, NIV

That's it. Not religious traditions or styles of worship. Not even debates over doctrine.

Love God. Love people.

Rerouting My Thinking is simply trusting God.

Wisdom begins with fearing God. And fearing God goes hand-in-hand with trusting Him. The more you trust God, the easier it is to reroute your thinking. When you truly believe in His promises, fear loses its power.

Many Christians never renew their minds enough to fully trust God. They live in survival mode, never experiencing the peace, joy, and growth that come from total dependence on Him.

But we don't have to live a life ruled by threats. With God, we can overcome isolation and broken relationships—and find peace in every area of our lives.

When we reroute our thinking, we discover that life isn't nearly as difficult as we often make it.

<< ACTION STEP >>

Think of a situation that feels threatening to you right now. Is it possible there's another story—another perspective—besides the one that threatens you? Write it down.

The rest of the RELATE process will teach you the action steps you need to restore your prefrontal cortex to normal and how to operate in those moments of threat.

<< QUESTIONS TO REFLECT ON >>

- When you feel threatened or upset, what is the first story you tend to tell yourself about what's happening?

- Can you recall a time when your first reaction made a situation worse? What might have changed if you had paused to reroute your thinking?

- In what ways have your thoughts created unnecessary fear, anxiety, or conflict in your relationships?

- Are there areas of your life where you're assuming the worst about others without knowing the full truth?

RELATE

- How would your life and relationships change if you consistently chose to replace fear with courage and truth?

- What one small step can you take today to begin practicing the habit of rerouting your thinking?

CHAPTER 4

"E" Elevate Others

Jesus made it clear that in His Kingdom, greatness is found in elevating others—not in seeking status or even survival.

Opportunities to elevate others come to us throughout the day. But what does that look like? Is He calling you to be walked on? Or does He want your life to revolve around someone else's agenda or needs? God wants you to discover the driving conviction and motivation behind life and relationships. That understanding will help you navigate the difference between the daily demands of others and the daily opportunities to elevate others.

Elevating Others Because They Belong to Him

People belong to God. Everyone belongs to God.

Your greatest value comes from how you behave toward God and people. Love is the goal.

If you were the only person left on earth, how valuable would your life really be? In one sense, you'd be the most valuable person in the world—literally! But in an even more sobering reality, you wouldn't have any value at all. There would be no one to love. Love makes you significant. Acts of love make you meaningful. Elevating others is the beginning of your attempt to love someone, especially when you are in a moment of threat.

Jesus taught that everything you do for others, you do for Him (Matthew 25). He was the ultimate example of elevating others, never using people for His own gain or pleasure. Even as He was brutally beaten and crucified, He decided others were worth dying for.

Our perception of being important is to be on top—like the top of a pyramid with everyone beneath us. But Jesus taught that the greatest among us is the servant of all (Matthew 23:11). Imagine a pyramid turned upside down, with the greatest one at the bottom, holding the rest up. That's what it means to elevate others. That's what it means to take on responsibility—to hold others up. Why? Because they belong to God.

One day, Jesus and the disciples were traveling, and along the way, there was a dispute among them. Jesus could see they were frustrated with each other, but they kept their distance from Him while they argued.

> *They came to Capernaum. When He was in the house, He asked them, "What were you arguing about on the road?" But they kept quiet because on the way they had argued about who was the greatest. Sitting down, Jesus called the Twelve and said, "Anyone who wants to be first must be the very last, and the servant of all." He took a little child whom He placed among them. Taking the child in His arms, He said to them, "Whoever welcomes one of these little children in My name welcomes Me; and whoever welcomes Me does not welcome Me but the One who sent Me."*
> – Mark 9:33-37 NIV

Elevate the weak. Elevate God's beloved. Elevate the children.

Elevate the poor. Elevate the orphans and widows. Even elevate your enemy. Pray for them. Lift them up.

I recall a conversation I once had with a woman who recounted how horrible someone had been to her throughout her life. She couldn't express enough how badly this woman had treated her over the years. I asked her if she had prayed for her. With great shock and disbelief that I would even suggest it, she said, "Why would I pray for her?! She doesn't deserve an ounce of God's blessing!"

What she didn't understand is that praying for our enemies isn't a prayer for God to bless them; it's a prayer for God to get a hold of them and, hopefully, bring them into the Kingdom.

Elevation doesn't always mean giving someone what they want or think they need. Elevating is much more. We must remember that Jesus came and physically showed us how to do relationships His way. He elevated everyone individually, differently. For some, He elevated them by being a friend—loving them, caring for them, healing them. For others, He elevated them by teaching them, believing they were teachable. For many who were living lives of dishonesty and sin, He became their friend and led them out of that life. And for those proudly steeped in religion and culture, He challenged them—very bluntly at times—to humble themselves and leave that life to follow Him.

This was a central part of what Jesus had been teaching the disciples. In John's gospel, we see that Jesus told them:

"Remember how I told you that servants are not greater than their master." – John 15:20 CEV

Clearly, the disciples already knew Jesus' values—that's why they tried to keep their argument hidden from Him. But Jesus wanted them to understand that God is deeply concerned with how we treat others. While all other religions emphasize how people treat their gods, the God of the Bible is concerned with how we treat other people. Jesus calls us to willingly put our own lives and reputations on the line for others. Why? Because God loves them, and they belong to Him.

Everything changes when you see people as belonging to God. Your spouse is His child. That difficult person at your church or workplace belongs to Him. The server at the restaurant—they aren't just someone bringing you food; they are a child of the King who should be treated with love and dignity.

When Christians start treating people as though they are accountable to God for how they interact with them, the world will take notice. People will see the true message of salvation. We are saved to serve. Elevating others is God's idea.

When a server spills something in your lap by accident, how do you react? Do you elevate them? Maybe if you're at an expensive restaurant. But what about at a cheap buffet? Well-known psychologist Dr. Jordan Peterson tells the story of a woman who haggled the price of eggs from a street vendor, driving the price down to $2.00 for a half dozen. Then she met a friend at a fancy restaurant and paid full price, even leaving a huge tip. Why? What motivates us to lord over those we consider "less" and want to impress those we consider "better"?

Our motive must always be to love people as Jesus does—elevating them.

One of the most sobering moments a husband or wife can

experience is realizing their spouse belongs to God. Every word, every gesture, every put-down—anything but love—is accountable to God.

As you move into this step in the RELATE process, the challenge is to thoughtfully look at the threat you are facing and begin to elevate anyone involved considering the reality that they belong to God.

When you feel a negative emotion because of someone else—whether it's their words, actions, or even just because they walked into the room—your responsibility is to turn your attention to the fact that they belong to your Master. He died for them.

The Apostle Paul, trying to instill the heart of Jesus into the early church, wrote:

> *"Christ encourages you, and his love comforts you; Don't be jealous or proud but be humble and consider others more important than yourselves. Care about them as much as you care about yourselves and think the same way that Christ Jesus thought: Christ was*

truly God. But he did not try to remain equal with God. Instead, he gave up everything and became a slave when he became like one of us." – Phil. 2:1, 3-7 CEV

Elevating Others is Challenging Others

Another form of elevating others is challenging them to be all that God made them to be. Paul wrote:

"Instead, speaking the truth in love, we will grow to become in every respect the mature body of him who is the head, that is, Christ." – Ephesians 4:15 NIV

Telling "the truth in love" helps someone rise and be better. God wants us to live above instincts and survival mode. Animalistic behavior is far beneath His people. He wants us to live like eternal beings with meaning—because that is who we are as His followers.

Paul was challenging followers of Jesus to rise to the expectations God had for them. He called them to maturity. He said, "We must stop acting like children" (Eph. 4:14-16 MSG). In other words, while everyone else acts like children, God expects

CHAPTER 4 - ELEVATE OTHERS

His people to grow up.

Jesus always called people to live beyond their fleshly instincts. He expected more from them. When the Pharisees threw a woman caught in adultery at His feet, He challenged them to show mercy. He didn't condemn the woman, but He also didn't excuse her choices. Up to that point, she had been living for herself and pursuing her own sinful desires. He said to her, "Go and sin no more" (John 8:11 NLT). He elevated her to pursue the same life He was living!

God created humans just below the angels (Hebrews 2:6-8). That means we are more than animals driven by survival and self-interest. Elevating others sometimes means expecting more from them—lovingly calling their greater self to rise.

If we truly believe people are created in God's image, we won't enable them to live selfishly or recklessly. Instead, we will challenge them to step into the life God designed for them.

Jesus didn't just teach this principle—He lived it. Though He was God, He humbled Himself and became a servant. He demonstrated that the way up is down, the way to lead is to serve, and the way to find life is to give it away.

When we elevate others, we reflect the heart of Christ. We become part of His plan to bring healing, restoration, and love into the world. And in the end, as Jesus promised, those who elevate others will be the greatest in His Kingdom.

Jesus taught us to do this by example. Even His own half-brothers didn't believe in Him—not until after the resurrection. When crowds began following Him and He claimed to be the Messiah, they thought He was taking things too far. The Bible doesn't give us all the details, but we do know that at one point, they tried to interrupt His ministry by using their position in His life.

> *"Someone told him, 'Your mother and brothers are standing outside, wanting to speak to you.' He replied, 'Who is my mother, and who are my brothers?' Pointing to his disciples, he said, 'Here are my mother and my brothers.'"* – Matt. 12:47-49 NIV

We don't have all the details of what His family was doing or why they were demanding Jesus leave the house, but we do know this: they had their own agenda for Him. They tried to use their relationship and position to get what they wanted. Jesus didn't give in to it.

You'll have people remind you, "I'm your mother…" "I'm your best friend…" "Oh, do it for your grandmother…" They will use their position to manipulate you from your purpose in life. It can feel confusing. Beware.

Many well-meaning Christians believe giving in to these demands is what Jesus would do. But a closer look at Jesus' life shows He had a clear mission and never allowed people to derail Him from it. He didn't waste time on those who only wanted to take from Him. In fact, Jesus often challenged people in ways that caused insincere people to leave.

At times, we deceitfully elevate people—not out of genuine love, but because it's easier to give them what they want than to deal with the conflict. We assume they will never grow, so we enable them rather than expecting more from them. Other times, we help because we fear the guilt of saying no. But when we look at these reasons honestly, we realize we aren't truly serving them—we're serving ourselves. Real help requires us to examine our motives first.

Before elevating someone, consider these questions:

- If I give my time, energy, or money, will my God-given responsibilities suffer?

- Am I truly helping them, or am I just trying to get them off my back or out of my way—making myself feel better?

- Is my "yes" to them a "no" to those God has assigned to me to elevate?

- Who else in my life will have to go without my time and resources?

- Who does God say is my responsibility?

- What kind of elevation does this person need? How can I serve or challenge them without enabling unhealthy behavior?

Remember, the true motive must be love—and love will be your guide. If you refrain from elevating someone by bringing

CHAPTER 4 - ELEVATE OTHERS

them to account, just to avoid feeling guilt for confronting them or not giving them what they want, they won't experience love. Your guilt isn't love. Guilt motivates us to be selfish. We will almost do anything we can to get rid of it. But true love always looks at what is best for others. There's a reason the answer is "no." Stick to it—if it is love.

I was speaking with a woman who was trying to get a grip on her fourteen-year-old niece. Her sister, the girl's mother, had died in a car accident, and she took the little girl in when she was only three. At lunch one Saturday, the girl came into the kitchen and made a sandwich. She used all the meat, stacking it high. Nobody said anything while she finished making it and sat down to eat. She took one bite, then got up, threw the rest in the trash, and left the room.

I began asking her questions about why she had allowed her niece to live like this. Eventually, she realized she felt so guilty that this little girl didn't have her mother all these years. She looked on with pity and tried to go easy on her. When she saw that she wasn't helping her niece—she was actually just helping herself—her whole perspective changed. She went home, immediately took charge of her home, and became a mother figure to her niece. Everything changed for everyone in that home that day.

When tempted to avoid elevating someone out of guilt, stop and remember your purpose and responsibility to love. Then, the negative emotion and anger you may feel toward them will fade. Sanity will be restored. It's then that you can relax and, with peace and confidence, say, "No, I can't do that for you."

Instead of enabling, it's time to elevate them. Treat them as human beings capable of change—created just a little lower than the angels.

Jesus gave us permission to set boundaries. He wasn't being unkind—He was showing wisdom. He never let anyone pull Him off mission. Neither should we.

Elevating Others is Having Compassion

Elevating others when you feel threatened by them begins with remembering that every person you encounter is threatened too. Everyone around you is processing threats (as you'll learn about in the next chapter), managing fears, and responding to stress in ways they may not even recognize—and that awareness changes everything. When you understand this, you can elevate others with compassion instead of frustration.

When the guy on the highway cuts you off, you can see it for what it is—his fight for survival, not a personal attack on you.

When your boss lashes out, it's their stress and pressure boiling over. When your child yells, "You're the worst parent in the world!", it's their own insecurity and immaturity talking. You don't have to react in anger. Instead, you can keep your sanity, recognizing that their behavior is driven by their own struggles, not by a calculated attempt to hurt you.

You never truly know what's going on in someone else's mind, but one thing is certain: everyone is processing threats. If your presence disrupts their mental autopilot and forces them to acknowledge something they'd rather not deal with, you become a perceived threat. People don't want to think deeply about their actions or motives—they prefer autopilot.

In our home, when teaching our kids to drive, we created an

exercise called Find the Threat. The goal was to point out any potential dangers on the road as soon as they sensed them.

Nearly every time their brain registered a threat, mine had already seen it too—whether it was a speeding car, a swerving truck, a heavily modified vehicle, or a reckless driver. It was a practical reminder that all of us, at all times, are scanning for threats and adjusting our actions accordingly.

Understanding this brings a shift in perspective. Everyone has a limbic system that is trying to manage threats. Some people have built walls to protect themselves from more pain. For some, that looks like anger. For others, it looks like being shy.

Some resort to being extroverted and controlling every room they walk into, while others stay away from new places and people altogether.

As you practice RELATE, instead of reacting emotionally, your instinct will be to begin to reroute your thinking and elevate others, knowing that they are all threatened too.

CHAPTER 4 - ELEVATE OTHERS

To embrace compassion means you won't let a rude driver, a grumpy boss, or a snappy comment control your entire day.

Jesus lived with this kind of compassion. Imagine Him and the disciples walking along a road, only to have a man on a camel ride by in a rush, yelling, "Get out of the way, you jobless hippies!" Can you picture Jesus shouting something back in anger? Of course not. He wasn't controlled by selfishness or offense.

In the previous story, when a group of religious leaders brought the woman caught in the act of adultery and threw her before Him, they treated her horribly. They humiliated her in front of the crowd and reminded Jesus that the Law of Moses required her to be stoned. They weren't interested in justice. They certainly weren't interested in her restoration. They wanted to trap Jesus with His own words.

They were trying to threaten Jesus. Would He let them threaten His social status? If He sided with the adulteress, it would make Him look immoral and ungodly. But instead of engaging in their game, Jesus rerouted His thinking and embraced compassion for her.

He knelt and began writing in the dirt. Then He stood up and said, "Let any one of you who is without sin be the first to throw a stone at her" (John 8:7 NIV).

While the religious leaders focused on punishing and condemning, Jesus elevated. Over and over, He was accused of eating with sinners, associating with tax collectors, and showing kindness to the outcasts of society. He even allowed a woman of questionable reputation to wash His feet with expensive perfume, equal to an entire year's wages. Some of

His own disciples were outraged, insisting that the money could have been used for the poor (Matthew 26:8-9).

Interestingly, in the very next verse, we read: Then Judas Iscariot went to the chief priests to betray Jesus for thirty pieces of silver (Matthew 26:14). For Judas, this moment shows that he didn't believe Jesus was the Messiah. Jesus' compassion didn't fit the mold of the king Judas wanted.

Yet, Jesus remained unmoved. He wasn't threatened by His

own reputation or by others' expectations. His only concern was elevating those who needed it most.

This is our model. Jesus elevated us when we didn't deserve it. He declared our significance—not because we earned it, but because He chose to give it. That means you and I are free to elevate others without fear of losing ourselves in the process. Our worth is secure in Christ.

Elevating Others Means Taking Care of Yourself

Elevating others is impossible if you aren't able. Can you give something you don't have? Can you spend time you don't have? Or grant someone something you don't have the authority to give? God's plan for each of us is to become like a tree planted by the water of life—healthy, strong, and able to bear much fruit (Jeremiah 17:8).

Elevating others doesn't mean neglecting yourself. The best way to elevate others is to first take care of yourself—to become strong enough to lift them up!

This can be difficult when you know others are in great

need, but you must remember that God is calling you to be His agent in other people's lives—by being loving, patient, and kind. These attributes must come from a genuine place of hope and peace within you. That kind of inner security can only be achieved when you have settled your faith on what God has said about your own needs and future.

Think about first responders. Firefighters don't rush into a burning building recklessly. Police officers don't draw their weapons carelessly. They stay calm and focused because they know their ability to help others depends on their own stability. Keeping your head and taking care of yourself is a service to those who need you.

The same principle applies in life. "Put your oxygen mask on first." It's part of the safety instructions given by flight attendants before every flight.

If you don't have financial stability, how can you help someone in need? If you neglect your health, how will you care for others? God's plan includes joy, peace, provision, and strength—not just for your sake, but so that you can share those blessings with others.

No, I'm not saying it's okay to push grandma out of the way to escape a burning building or to leave your kids behind when a shark swims nearby. The kind of selfishness that takes advantage of others or only looks out for yourself is never justified. Jesus said, "The greatest way to show love for friends is to die for them" (John 15:13 CEV). Sacrificing for others is noble—but so is living in a way that allows you to be dependable for them. A noble life is a stable life. It allows others to count on the commitments you've made to them.

We should strive to be the kind of person who is ready to lift others up, instant in season and out of season (2 Timothy 4:2). A parent who stays sober—just in case they need to drive their child or a friend to the ER in an emergency—is living a life set on elevating. Choosing a healthy lifestyle so your loved ones don't have to become caregivers or lose you too soon is a life of elevating. Saving money so you have enough to live on when you can't work anymore—not becoming a burden to others—is a life of elevating. True self-care isn't selfish—it's preparing yourself to be a blessing to others, for a long, healthy, meaningful life.

Sometimes, we do find ourselves in need, deeply wanting others to elevate us and give us a hand up. One of the keys to getting what you need is remembering that you've already been given seeds to find and elevate someone else. God has given you seed to sow. So how do you find it?

Jesus gave us this secret to sanity in those moments of desperation. When we feel like we have nothing to offer and all of our attempts to be strong seem futile, here's His formula for Kingdom success—a way to diagnose and prescribe spiritual medicine for yourself. He said:

> *"Here is a simple, rule-of-thumb guide for behavior: Ask yourself what you want people to do for you, then grab the initiative and do it for them."*
> – Matthew 7:12 MSG

When you need love, give love. When you feel insecure, offer security to someone else. When you long for encouragement, speak encouragement into another's life. This is how we fulfill

CHAPTER 4 - ELEVATE OTHERS

the command to elevate others.

Jesus wanted the world to love Him as God, so He loved like no one else ever could. He probably wasn't feeling much love from us when He was hanging on the cross—but He was certainly pouring it out to us.

God's command is simple: love God, love your neighbor as yourself. Do for others what you want them to do for you.

It's not hard to find someone who needs what you need. Too many people wander through life, unsure of their purpose, waiting for someone to tell them how they can contribute. But Jesus made it simple—just look inside yourself, find your need, and go meet that need in someone else's life.

The other day, I needed to hear that everything was going to be okay—that God was still working, that He always comes through. It was just one of those days. But no one was calling to tell me that. So, I picked up the phone and called someone else who I thought might need to hear it. By the time I hung up, I believed it too.

That's the power of elevating others. When you give what you need, you'll find that you had it all along.

There's another formula Jesus gave us for diagnosing and prescribing spiritual medicine for ourselves. This one has to do with dealing with your own sin before you attempt to elevate someone in a challenging way. Jesus said that when you see your friend commit a sin, before you even begin to deal with their sin, you should look at yourself first:

> *"Why do you look at the speck of sawdust in your brother's eye and pay no attention to the plank in your own eye? How can you say to your brother, 'Let me take the speck out of your eye,' when all the time there is a plank in your own eye? You hypocrite, first take the plank out of your own eye, and then you will see clearly to remove the speck from your brother's eye."*
> – Matthew 7:3-5 NIV

This passage is often misunderstood as simply saying, "don't judge." But let's look at it another way. Jesus does expect us to help and elevate others with their sin—but before we help, we must do some self-care and check our own heart: "First take the plank out of your own eye."

He's saying that before you try to help someone else, carefully make sure you have your own life in order. And in the next verse, He wisely reminds us that they may not be ready for your help, as we just discussed: "Do not give dogs what is sacred; do not throw your pearls to pigs. If you do, they may trample them under their feet and turn and tear you to pieces" (Matthew 7:6 NIV). Giving your service and goods (pearls) to someone who won't use them to move forward (swine) isn't wise.

The point is: take care of your sin first. Clean your own room before you try to clean up someone else's home. And sometimes, once you can see more clearly, you'll find your friend doesn't even have a problem. Do some self-care before you even begin trying to fix someone else.

You are responsible for you. Deal with yourself. Care for yourself.

<< QUESTIONS TO REFLECT ON >>

- Who should I elevate right now?

- If I can't, what is keeping me from being able to?

- Who in my life needs to be challenged to move forward, be better, and live the life God created them to live?

- What area(s) in my life do I need to apply self-care?

- Where am I weak?

- If I fix _____ in my life, then I can be a blessing to others.

- Have I falsely accused someone of something?

- Does that expose anything in me?

- What sin do I need to deal with in my own life?

- Who can I elevate with compassion?

CHAPTER 5

"L" List Your Threats

Many people struggle to go down this path because we don't like to admit we feel threatened. I hear a lot of pushback on the word "threat." For some reason, our culture sees it as a sign of weakness. Someone might say, "I don't like the way my boss talks down to me." But when asked how that threatens them, the response is often, "Oh no, I'm not threatened. I just don't like how she communicates."

But refusing to acknowledge your threats is like denying that you breathe. You might try to hide it, standing still, making sure no one sees your chest rise and fall. But everyone knows—you're alive, so you're breathing. In the same way, threats to the human brain are as natural and necessary as breathing. Without this function, you wouldn't have survived past toddlerhood. If you're living, you experience threats.

I was talking to a man very involved in his church but struggling in his marriage. He shared that his wife often spoke rudely to him, that they weren't as close as they used to be, and that they'd had a major fight the night before. He looked exhausted, his frustration evident as he spoke. He was open to working through "Reroute My Thinking" and "Elevate Others," but when we got to "List Your Threats," he immediately resisted. "No, I'm not threatened. I'm fine. She just needs to see what she's doing."

As a Christian, he needed some accountability in this moment.

I asked him, "Are you a Christian?"

"Yes, you know I am."

"If Jesus were sitting here listening to you talk, would He be more interested in what your wife is doing or what's happening in your heart?"

"Probably me."

CHAPTER 5 - LIST YOUR THREATS

"Can you change your wife?"

"No, I've tried that for the last nine years. Apparently not."

"Can you change you?"

"Yes, with God's help."

"Absolutely. But can you change if you don't know what needs to change?"

"Probably not."

"If you trust this process and do the work, you might see something in yourself that you've never seen before—something that could be the key to making the changes you need to make. Are you interested?"

"Yes."

"Then let's begin."

Over the next thirty minutes, God worked in this man's life, setting in motion a transformation in his marriage and other relationships. But he had to open himself to the possibility that he was wrong. Until we are free to be wrong, we will stubbornly stand on our soapbox, declaring ourselves right while the people we love pull further away.

Being "mostly right" means we're also "some wrong."

God wants to empower you to live above life's threats—even the threat of being wrong. But until you recognize and understand the threats you face, He can't. Thankfully, you don't need a degree in sociology to figure this out. It's actually simple—because all threats fall into just three categories.

There Are Only Three Threats in Life

Anytime you experience a negative emotion, you are experiencing a threat. And out of all the possible threats in life, every single one fits into one of these three categories:

1. **Security** – If your basic needs (food, water, money, home, air, etc.) are at risk or being taken away, your security is threatened.
2. **Social Status** – If you stand to lose a position or not attain one you desire (job title, spouse, parent, child,

place in line, etc.), or if you perceive yourself as less than someone else, your social status is threatened.

3. **Intimate Relationships** – If someone you love or rely on is being taken from you or chooses to leave, your intimate relationships are threatened.

Listing your threats is the mental work of identifying what your brain perceives as a danger. This process is an inventory. Instead of focusing on how others need to change to stop threatening you, the key is to pause and ask, "How am I being threatened?" Identifying your threats not only defines them but gives you a place to start in reclaiming peace and clarity.

More importantly, these threats often reveal areas where your faith in God is weak—so exploring them brings significant spiritual growth.

My Threats Are About Me

Your threats are about your security, your social status, and your intimate relationships. We are all wired for self-preservation, yet we often don't realize it. At a funeral, for instance, we assume we are grieving because we miss the deceased. But deep down, our brain is also contemplating our own mortality.

Seeing a beggar on a street corner, you might feel compelled to give them a dollar, believing it's an act of compassion. But is it possible that your brain fears you might end up in their position one day? Sometimes hidden fears—not pure humanitarian motives—drive our actions. Our threats shape us and motivate us in ways we don't always recognize.

The great danger is that we think we are acting in love, the highest and purest motive we can achieve. All the while, we are operating from a very base level of reasoning.

The point is that your threats are rooted in your instinct for self-preservation. It's easy to disguise them with nobler motives, but that only blinds us to reality. A hidden or misidentified motive can cause significant damage, which is why it's crucial to uncover them.

My Threats Are About God

If I don't truly believe that God has secured my future—forever—then I will fight desperately to protect what I have here. The same applies when I don't trust what He says about my social status or relationships.

This is where clarity returns. I love seeing this moment in a RELATE session—the point where someone's stress, pain, or confusion suddenly lifts. Their countenance changes, their prefrontal cortex engages, and peace settles in. The turning point comes when they answer three questions:

1. What has God said about your security?
2. What has God said about your social status?
3. What has God said about your intimate relationships?

When people begin recalling what they've read in the Bible or heard from their pastor, their faith activates, and relief follows. Hope floods in as they remember God's promises. I've seen people shift from anguish to peace in a matter of moments simply because they remembered what God has already assured them.

Whatever threatens you reveals where you lack trust in God.

As a Christian, I can speak from experience—these three

areas always point back to faith.

I once met an atheist struggling with severe stress. His father had been an atheist, his parents' divorce had been ugly, and now both were gone. His work environment was tense, his relationships were strained, and emotionally, he was a wreck.

As we worked through RELATE, he was amazed at how quickly and simply we identified his struggles.

"I've been to so many counselors, spent countless hours and who knows how much money, but no one ever gave me this," he said. "This is incredible."

I replied, "Yes, but here's the problem. This is as far as you can go with me. The rest of the process is only effective when you are willing to explore who God is and how trusting Him changes everything. So, if you ever want to know more, let me know."

People try everything to manage their threats—pets, alcohol, medication, entertainment, distractions—anything to ease the stress for a moment. But when those solutions fail, the good

CHAPTER 5 - LIST YOUR THREATS

news is that Jesus is still there, waiting.

For the Christian, here's how this applies:

- **Security:** If you fear losing your job, you've forgotten that God has prepared an eternal home for you. If you fear losing what you have or missing out on something you want, remember that He has promised everything to you for eternity.

- **Social Status:** If you worry about someone taking your place, you've forgotten that you are God's child, His partner, and His friend. If God is for you, who can be against you? Your worth is not in titles or public opinion; it is written on the palm of His hand.

- **Intimate Relationships:** If you fear that someone you love will leave or be taken from you, you've forgotten that God has promised an eternal family and lasting relationships beyond this life.

God's truth will always outlast your threats. When you trust in Him, your threats lose their power. And when your threats lose their power, you are finally free to live—and you begin to build relationships with unshakable trust.

God Knows About These Threats

Jesus understood that people live by their threats. He recognized that the people around Him were operating from a place of fear, driven by their own personal threats. They wanted Him to be their king, to overthrow Rome and restore the Jewish kingdom. But Jesus didn't engage with them on their terms (John 2:23-25). He remained focused on His mission, knowing that people's motives were often shaped by their struggles and failures.

God is fully aware of this human condition. Think about it—whenever an angel appeared in the Bible, their first words were often, "Do not fear!" In other words, "Don't be afraid! I come with good news. I am not a threat. Don't let fear take over!" God knows this is going on in us, and Jesus modeled the right way for us to live—not only in His life but even in His death.

CHAPTER 5 - LIST YOUR THREATS

These Threats Are My Responsibility

When you take responsibility for your own threats and recognize how you might be threatening others, your relationships can drastically improve.

You are responsible for managing your own threats. Unchecked threats lead to bitterness, anger, conflict, and destruction. They can also take a toll on your health. Studies have linked negative emotions to various diseases, and prolonged stress can lead to depression. Research suggests that long-term prefrontal cortex shrinkage—often a result of unresolved threats—can contribute to depression. If you find yourself struggling, it may be worth considering whether unresolved threats are playing a role. You may find that recognizing and addressing your threats, which enlarges the prefrontal cortex, could help you experience greater mental and emotional freedom.

Managing your threats is one of your God-given responsibilities. Jesus demonstrated this in the ultimate way—by carrying His cross. His sacrifice was an example of how we are called to do the same daily.

> "Whoever wants to be my disciple must deny themselves and take up their cross daily and follow me."
> – Luke 9:23 NIV

Obviously, Jesus was speaking figuratively here. We can't physically die every day, but we are called to die to ourselves. Learning to let go of our own needs and self-preservation instincts is the key to freedom and healthy relationships.

Threat-Free Living is Peace and Joy

The people who have the most fun riding roller coasters are the ones with their arms raised in the air, letting go of their need to control. Life is similar in that we are on this ride whether we like it or not. The only way to enjoy it is to surrender control and trust God. To die daily, as Jesus put it, you must:

- Surrender your need for security to God.

- Let God define your identity and position.

- Trust Him to provide the relationships you need.

When we release these concerns, we experience true freedom.

We see an example of this in the story of a father who brought his demon-possessed son to Jesus. The boy had suffered from possession since childhood, often being thrown into fire or water. Desperate, the father asked Jesus, "If you can do anything, have compassion on us and help us" (Mark 9:22 NKJV).

It's significant that the man said, "...have compassion on us and help us" rather than just asking for his son. He recognized that his child's suffering affected the entire family.

Jesus responded, "'If you can'?... Everything is possible for one who believes" (Mark 9:23 NIV).

The father, in one of the most honest prayers recorded in scripture, said, "I do believe; help me overcome my unbelief" (Mark 9:24 NIV). And Jesus healed his son.

The only reason we feel threatened is because of our unbelief. Unbelief comes from not knowing. But God doesn't want us to just believe—He wants us to KNOW. This father was essentially saying, "I believe, but help me to KNOW."

Belief is a choice, but knowledge is unshakable. A child who is told the stove is hot may still reach out to touch it. But once they experience the burn, they *know*, and no one can convince them otherwise.

God wants us to KNOW Him. He wants us to experience Him so deeply that we no longer live in fear.

You Are Responsible for Recognizing How You Threaten Others

Have you noticed how people tend to speak kindly about even the most difficult individuals after they've passed away? The moment someone breathes their last, they are no longer a threat. Suddenly, people start recalling their good qualities, even if they were few.

The reality is that you, too, are a potential threat to those around you. Your choices impact others in ways you may not even realize. You decide how fast people can drive behind you. You determine where others can park. You influence how much intimacy your spouse experiences. You control how much time people get to spend with you. Even small actions can be threatening.

In high school, I had two friends who were identical twins, and they both drove identical white Chevy Corvairs. Every day on their way home from school, they would drive side by side at 35 mph, blocking traffic and refusing to let anyone pass. At the time, we thought it was hilarious. But looking back, I can only imagine how much frustration they caused for the hundreds of drivers stuck behind them every day. How many of those drivers took that anger home? How many arguments or ruined evenings stemmed from their actions? We rarely realize how much our everyday behavior impacts others—let alone the things we knowingly do that annoy or hurt people.

Whether it's honking, yelling, making faces, or giving someone the silent treatment, people are constantly communicating their frustrations. Are you listening? Many of these reactions are the direct result of decisions we make—decisions we can control.

That means we have the power to improve our relationships simply by being more intentional.

This is exactly what Jesus was talking about when He gave us the Golden Rule. But in this context, it is: don't do to others what you don't want them to do to you.

Most of the time, we don't intend to be a threat to others. We just don't think about it. But the reality is that everyone around us has an active limbic system—a natural defense mechanism that reacts to perceived threats. Without using RELATE, their default response will often be to blame, reject, and not trust you.

One of the greatest steps you can take in improving relationships is identifying how you might be threatening others—whether intentionally or not—and making changes to remove those threats. If leaving the toilet seat up is a problem, start putting it down. If you drive too fast, slow down. If you gossip, stop. If you withhold something that others need, take care of it. You'd be amazed how small adjustments can lead to major improvements in your relationships. When they can physically see that you care, even a little, it goes a long way.

A classic example comes from the movie *The Three Amigos*, one of my favorite movies. In one scene, Steve Martin, Martin Short, and Chevy Chase are crossing a desert when they stop for water. Steve Martin's canteen is completely empty. Martin Short tips his canteen up and gets a mouthful of sand. But Chevy Chase? His canteen is overflowing. He takes a big swig, gargles, spits it out, then dumps the rest on the ground—right in front of his desperate friends. To top it off, he casually applies lip balm and asks, "Lip balm?"

Hilarious in a movie. But in real life? Not so funny.

Every day, you are surrounded by people who desperately need what you have in abundance—kindness, eternal life, hope, encouragement, time, help, love. They need to be recognized. When we ignore or withhold from those around us, we create unnecessary barriers in our relationships. But when we remove the threats we pose to others, we create an opening to better relationships!

I once counseled a 14-year-old boy named Bobby who was

distraught. I asked him, "Bobby, is there anything you want to talk about?"

"My dad and I are always fighting. He gets so mad at me all the time," Bobby said.

"What does he get mad about?" I asked.

"He's always telling me to clean my room. I just don't understand why we can't get along."

I smiled and said, "I have something to tell you that is so profound. What I'm about to tell you is going to change everything if you will hear me and do it. It will totally repair your relationship with your dad. Are you ready?"

His eyes lit up. "Yes!"

"Here it is, man. Go home and clean your room."

He looked at me as if that option had never occurred to him. But he walked out of that church like a man on a mission. Two weeks later, his mom stopped me with tears in her eyes. "John, I don't know what you said to Bobby, but everything in our home has changed. Thank you."

Most of the time, we know how we are threatening the people around us because they are telling us. People are communicating there's a problem. Are you listening? Do you care? It's time to listen and respond.

Bobby made a small change that had a profound impact. And what's even more significant? Within the next ten years, his father passed away. I doubt Bobby ever regretted the effort he made to strengthen that relationship.

So ask yourself: Is your boss really asking too much? What about your spouse? Your parents? Your pastor? Your friends? God? Some things are just simple fixes. If you don't wear deodorant, don't expect people to want to be close to you—seriously. If you don't shower regularly, people will avoid you. It's not a mystery. And yet, some people refuse to make the most basic adjustments that would dramatically improve their interactions with others.

It's easy to point the finger at others, but what about you? What small, simple changes could you make to remove the threats you pose to those around you? Maybe it's eliminating one negative word from your vocabulary. Maybe it's learning to be flexible instead of always controlling the plans.

Or maybe, the issue runs deeper. Perhaps an addiction is threatening your relationships. If you ask the people left in your wake, they'll tell you—your addiction is more important to you than they are. Or maybe you have a problem with authority, refusing to follow direction unless it was your idea. That's a quick way to lose jobs and strain relationships. I would even argue that many struggling marriages today are just one simple decision away from becoming great and happy marriages.

Removing the threats you create in your relationships is part of your responsibility.

<< ACTION STEP >>

Think of a relationship struggle that is happening right now. Answer these questions:

1. **Reroute My Thinking** – Is there another way to view this situation that isn't so threatening?

2. **Elevate Others** – Who do I need to lift up? They belong to God, and I am accountable to Him for how I treat them.

3. **List Your Threats** – Identify specific ways I may be threatening others and what God says about each area:

    o **Security:** _____
    _____

    o **Social Status:** _____
    _____

    o **Intimate Relationships:** _____
    _____
    _____

God's wisdom offers clarity on how we should treat others. Are you listening?

RELATE

<< QUESTIONS TO REFLECT ON >>

- When was the last time you reacted negatively to someone? What threat might you have been feeling in that moment—security, social status, or relationship?

- Do you tend to deny feeling threatened? How has that denial impacted your relationships?

- Can you think of a situation where being "mostly right" actually hurt your relationship with someone?

- How does your trust in God change when you feel threatened? What has God said about your security, status, or relationships that you need to remember?

- What are some small, practical changes you could make today to remove unnecessary threats to those around you?

- Have you ever dismissed or ignored someone's attempt to tell you how your behavior is affecting them? How could listening differently improve that relationship?

CHAPTER 6

"A" Accept Your Part

It's time to take the next step and own your part. Now that you've recognized how you were threatened—and that you didn't believe God in that moment—it's time to take an honest look at what you've created by trying to fix the threat using the wrong tools.

Anytime you don't reroute your thinking and bring your threats to God, your flesh will automatically try to fix them with destructive tools. Imagine going to a dentist who has the wrong tools. You look over at the tray and see a hammer, a chisel, some firecrackers, and a little spackling to fill your teeth. That's the kind of toolset we often use to deal with our threats!

In Christian teaching, there's a list called *The Seven Deadly Sins*. They're called deadly because they destroy. They kill relationships. They keep us stuck. Let's take a closer look at each of them.

Pride

Pride is the mother of all the other sins. Every sin begins with pride. Pride tells me I deserve more, better, greater, and bigger than what I'm getting. Pride convinces me I have the right to use all the other sins to remedy the problems in my life. *I deserve to get angry. I deserve to lust. I deserve to be a glutton.* And so on.

Pride blinds us. It keeps us from seeing the truth. It gives us permission to destroy our lives and relationships.

But let me ask you—has your pride ever given you peace, contentment, or hope? Has it ever brought you closer to someone?

Anger

Anger hides behind a good desire for justice, deceiving us into thinking it's okay to use because it's "for a good cause."

But anger is a shortcut. Instead of taking the long, hard route to repair a relationship, we use anger to get everyone back in line quickly. And in doing so, we often pair it with another deadly sin—*sloth*. Instead of doing the real work to restore a relationship, we choose the shortcut of anger.

Here's how it works: pride comes first. Pride tells me, *You don't have time for this,* or *You'll look like a doormat if you don't deal with this now.* Those thoughts fuel emotions, which suddenly burst into flames. And now, instead of resolving the situation, we lash out.

But has your anger ever fixed a relationship long-term?

Lust

Lust is another shortcut—and sloth is usually hiding behind it. Lust offers a counterfeit version of love. But real love is about giving yourself to someone; lust is about possessing someone.

It's the difference between God and Satan. In Scripture, when Satan occupies someone, it's called possession. God, on the other hand, gives Himself to us in love—He never forces Himself on us.

Lust uses people for our own pleasure without giving anything in return. It's a one-sided illusion.

This is why marriage matters. Marriage is about giving yourself to your spouse and becoming an extension of one another. It's not about owning or using your spouse—it's about caring for them. Paul reminded the early church of this:

> *"Husbands and wives should be fair with each other about having sex. A wife belongs to her husband instead of to herself, and a husband belongs to his wife instead of to himself. So don't refuse sex to each other, unless you agree not to have sex for a little while, in order to spend time in prayer. Then Satan won't be able to tempt you because of your lack of self-control."*
> – 1 Corinthians 7:3–5 CEV

Lust wants the benefits of love without the cost. It devalues the person you desire.

Has lust ever truly filled your need to be loved, wanted, and desired?

Greed

Greed is about stockpiling security. It leads to lying, cheating, and other destructive behaviors—all in an attempt to make your present peaceful by making your future brighter. But instead, it only creates anxiety.

When you struggle to believe what God says about your future, you'll try to take matters into your own hands. The more you get, the more you want. The bigger your stockpile, the more protective you become.

Has greed ever left you satisfied, content, and hopeful?

Gluttony

Gluttony says, *I'm going to get all I can while I can.* It's rooted in our instinct for pleasure.

We often think of gluttony as overeating, but it can touch many areas of life. When I do an ounce of work, pride tells me I deserve a ton of pleasure. When I experience an ounce of pain, I feel like I deserve two tons of comfort. Gluttony is often used to soothe our flesh instead of turning to God.

It also robs us of the moment. Instead of savoring what we have, we consume without restraint, always thinking about the next indulgence.

When my kids were young, we had movie nights. The plan was simple: popcorn, M&M's, and a good movie. But sometimes, we wasted the entire night trying to decide what to watch. We missed the moment because we were searching for the "perfect" experience. Looking back, we would give anything to sit and watch *any* movie again with their late mother.

Gluttony destroys the moment that could have been enough.

Has gluttony ever solved your problem for more than a few hours?

Envy

Envy looks at what someone else has and says, *I want that*. Pride tells us we deserve it more than they do. We question

God—*Why don't I have that?*

Envy leads to shortcuts like anger or lust to get what others have worked for. It divides relationships and keeps us from appreciating others' success.

You must remember that God created you with purpose. Envy makes you question His design and intentions. It convinces you to carry a chip on your shoulder, feeling slighted by God.

Has envy ever brought you closer to peace or contentment?

Sloth

Sloth isn't just laziness—it's avoiding responsibility. It's failing to do what's needed to fix a problem or build a healthy relationship.

When you consistently use shortcuts like anger or lust, sloth is hiding behind them. It's easier to react than to do the hard work of love, communication, and commitment.

Sloth is fueled by pride. Pride tells us, *Life shouldn't be this hard. Marriage shouldn't be this much work. Raising kids shouldn't take this much effort.* It deceives us into thinking we've already done enough.

I've seen it time and again—older people who flip a "deserve switch." They stop investing in relationships and demand respect without giving it. They believe they've done enough, and the world owes them now. But this mindset pushes people away, and loneliness sets in.

When has sloth ever provided a lasting reward in your life?

How to Accept Your Part

At this point in the RELATE process, the key question is:

Which one or more of these seven deadly sins have I been using to fix my problem?

For every vice, there is a virtue. Instead of using sin to fix your threats, you can use virtue instead. Virtues don't always fix the problem—but they keep you from making it worse. They help you make things right, as much as it depends on you.

- For pride, there's humility *(modesty, meekness).*

- For anger, there's patience *(forbearance, calmness)*.

- For lust, there's chastity *(purity, self-respect)*.

- For greed, there's charity *(generosity, selflessness)*.

- For gluttony, there's temperance *(self-control, moderation)*.

- For envy, there's kindness *(goodwill, compassion)*.

- For sloth, there's diligence *(perseverance, responsibility)*.

Trying to stop sinning as a way to fix your threats is a lifetime of work—and ultimately, a losing battle. But God calls us to something more. He calls us to love. When you love, sin has no place to operate.

God hasn't left a vacuum in us where sin once lived. He invites us to live differently, to live in love. That's exactly what Jesus taught. The Old Covenant was all about *"Thou shalt not..."* The New Covenant is about *"Thou shalt."*

"Teacher, which is the greatest commandment in the Law?"

Jesus replied: "'Love the Lord your God with all your heart and with all your soul and with all your mind.' This is the first and greatest commandment. And the second is like it: 'Love your neighbor as yourself.' All the Law and the Prophets hang on these two commandments."
– Matthew 22:35–40 NIV

When we love God and love people, we naturally stop sinning—and we experience the eternal power of love. So much of your life has been wasted trying not to do bad when you've actually been set free to do good.

God isn't calling you to self-restraint—He's calling you to self-expression through love.

Entitlement Has Everything to Do with Your Part

We hold on to offenses because it feels like an easy payday. We believe we are entitled or *deserve* something when others offend us. If your spouse says something hurtful—you deserve. If your coworker snaps at you—you deserve. If your neighbor's dog messes up your yard—you deserve.

Your flesh craves for others to owe you. And when you feel that you deserve something, you'll convince yourself that sin is justified.

Think about the last time you gave in to your favorite hidden sin. How did you get there? What made you think it was okay?

For example, my favorite snack cake is the Tastykake Bells. When they stopped making them after Covid, I had stashes hidden in my office and bedroom. I would create a problem, or make something negative bigger than it was, just to feel justified in eating one. My brain tricked me into feeling like I deserved it.

This is how the flesh works. A man who wants to feed his lust will create conflict with his wife, so he feels justified. A woman who wants to drink after work will find a reason to deserve it. We create problems to justify our sin.

The flesh is constantly scheming to get what it wants. And when others hurt or offend us, we often turn to sin to fix the threat. But deserve has everything to do with it.

RELATE

Your Part Is a New Life Focus

Jesus didn't invite you to spend your life trying not to sin. He invited you to love. Every time you use sin to fix your threats, you miss an opportunity to love.

That's why God shifted the focus from *Thou shalt not* to *Thou shalt*. From avoiding sin to actively loving.

When I love my neighbor, I'm not going to murder him, envy him, or covet what he has. When I love God, I won't worship idols or take His name in vain. Love fulfills the law.

1 Corinthians 13 gives us the clearest picture of our mission:

Love is patient, love is kind. It does not envy, it does not boast, it is not proud. It does not dishonor others, it is not self-seeking, it is not easily angered, it keeps no record of wrongs.

Love does not delight in evil but rejoices with the truth. It always protects, always trusts, always hopes, always perseveres.

Love never fails. But where there are prophecies, they will cease; where there are tongues, they will be stilled; where there is knowledge, it will pass away.

For we know in part and we prophesy in part, but when completeness comes, what is in part disappears.

When I was a child, I talked like a child, I thought like a child, I reasoned like a child. When I became a man, I put the ways of childhood behind me.

For now we see only a reflection as in a mirror; then we shall see face to face. Now I know in part; then I shall know fully, even as I am fully known.

> *"And now these three remain: faith, hope and love. But the greatest of these is love."* – 1 Cor. 13:4–13 NIV

Jesus never commanded you to go out and *be loved*. His command was to go and *love*.

Because He took care of your eternal threats, you are now free to forget about them and focus on doing His work every day.

RELATE

<< ACTION STEP >>

Look back at the action you took in the previous chapter and decide what your part is. How have you been trying to fix the threat(s) with sin? Ask yourself:

What sin(s) am I using to deal with my threats?

- Pride

- Anger

- Lust

- Greed

- Gluttony

- Envy

- Sloth

CHAPTER 6 - ACCEPT YOUR PART

<< QUESTIONS TO REFLECT ON >>

- Which of the Seven Deadly Sins do you recognize in how you've tried to fix other threats in your life?

- Has pride ever helped you feel more at peace or brought healing to a relationship?

- In what ways has anger created more damage than resolution in your relationships?

- Have you ever chased lust, greed, or gluttony only to feel emptier afterward?

- How has envy affected your ability to appreciate others and be content with your own life?

- Are there areas of your life where you've taken shortcuts (sloth) instead of doing the hard, right thing?

- What would it look like for you to replace these destructive patterns with virtues like humility, patience, kindness, and love?

CHAPTER 7

"T" Turn From Your Sin to God

Now that you've identified your part, you have something meaningful to bring to God—something He is interested in hearing. Instead of focusing on what everyone else is doing wrong, imagine how much it would delight God if you started talking to Him about your own sin.

We struggle to deal with our own sin, let alone the sin we see in others. Should we judge it? Ignore it? Challenge it? The reason we often don't know how to respond is that our understanding of love is skewed. We've also forgotten that our first responsibility is to God.

CHAPTER 7 - TURN FROM YOUR SIN TO GOD

Your First Responsibility is to God

Father God, who are You? What do You like? And what don't You like? I want to know You and accommodate You in my life. Those are the words of true salvation—relationship.

After David committed adultery and then murder to cover it up, he came to a moment of deep repentance and recorded his painful confession in Psalm 51:

> *"Wash away all my iniquity and cleanse me from my sin. For I know my transgressions, and my sin is always before me. Against you, you only, have I sinned and done what is evil in your sight; so you are right in your verdict and justified when you judge."*
> – Psalm 51:2-4 NIV

Some interpret this to mean that when we sin, we only need to repent to God. But if we take the whole of Scripture into account, we realize that most of the sins we commit against God involve hurting others. And if we sin against God by harming others, wouldn't it stand to reason that when we reconcile with those we've wronged, we are also reconciling with God?

Yet, our first step must be to turn to God—acknowledging that He sees everything and is willing to help us make things right.

Jesus reinforced this truth. In Matthew 5:24, He said that if you come to worship and realize you've wronged someone, you should leave immediately and make things right first. That's because your first duty is to obey God—and God says that making things right with others is the priority.

Turning from your sin to God means handling your sin His way. If you stole something, return it. If you spread lies about someone, go tell the truth. Jesus made it clear in Matthew 25 that what we do to others, we do to Him. So, if we harm others, we have also harmed Jesus. And God's way is to make it right.

This is not karma. We aren't talking about some unknown force balancing the scales of the universe. We are talking about a real, living God who knows even the smallest details of our lives.

Some people look at the universe and think, "There's no way a God that big could care about us." But others look at it and say, "Wow, God must be really big! Big enough to know everything—even how many hairs are on my head!" Jesus said He does know that number, at all times. That's how personal He is.

Because He is that personal, He does not overlook our sin or the pain we cause. As Abel's blood cried out to God for justice (Genesis 4:10), so do the injustices of the world.

What if David's prayer was more literal than we realize? What if God really does keep track of every tear, every sorrow?

> *"Don't let them get away with their wickedness; in your anger, O God, bring them down. You keep track of all my sorrows. You have collected all my tears in your bottle. You have recorded each one in your book."*
> – Psalm 56:7-8 NLT

God takes sin seriously. He sees the destruction it brings to our lives and relationships. But His response is not just judgment—it's love. And when we apply His love to our sin, we gain clarity about how to deal with it.

A Higher Calling Than Sin Management

Paul understood this deeply. He wrote:

RELATE

"Think of us as servants of Christ who have been given the work of explaining God's mysterious ways. And since our first duty is to be faithful to the One we work for, it doesn't matter to me if I am judged by you or even by a court of law. In fact, I don't judge myself." – 1 Corinthians 4:1-3 CEV

Paul is teaching us that there are far more important things to get done in the Kingdom of God than simply dealing with sin. He made a conscious decision to focus his time and attention on faithfully working for Jesus—not wasting his life trying to look innocent to the eyes of others. Their judgment meant nothing to him.

Many people in the church get stuck in a mindset of sin avoidance. They see their faith as a constant struggle to stay holy. But God's plan is far greater than just turning from sin—He calls us to turn to Him and embrace a life of love.

Paul frequently addressed the issue of "weak-conscience" Christians who elevated minor issues to matters of faith. In 1 Corinthians 8–10, he lays out a key principle: We are free to live in love, but we are not free to flaunt our freedom.

For example, throughout church history, people have created hard rules about what a "real Christian" should or shouldn't do. Some have boycotted companies, treated Christmas trees or Halloween as sinful, or insisted that true Christians should only listen to Christian music and never watch secular movies.

Religious legalism creeps in when people elevate personal convictions into universal commands. Paul addressed this by using the example of food offered to idols.

He wrote that eating food offered to idols is completely harmless. But not everyone agreed. He then instructed us that if we are with someone who believes it is wrong to eat food offered to idols—someone he calls "weak in conscience"—then we shouldn't eat it. Just skip the meal if you have to, so you don't cause that person to stumble.

Paul wasn't trying to be offensive. He taught us how to show God's love for others. He clarifies this when he writes:

> *"I have the right to do anything," you say—but*

> *not everything is beneficial. "I have the right to do anything"—but not everything is constructive. No one should seek their own good, but the good of others. Eat anything sold in the meat market without raising questions of conscience."* – 1 Cor. 10:23-25 NIV

Paul is applying the blood of Jesus to sin, making sin a matter of relationship rather than legalism. He raises the standard beyond what even the Law required—just as Jesus did in the Sermon on the Mount (Matthew 5:21-48). That standard is love.

Here's what that looks like: If a Christian with a weaker conscience is struggling with a particular issue, I must be careful not to parade my freedom in Christ.

For example, like the man I mentioned earlier in the book who became angry over the version of the Bible I was using. Out of love, I was willing to set that version aside until he grew in his understanding. However, when he demanded that I agree with him—that my Bible version was from the devil—I couldn't accommodate. At that point, he had a choice to make.

Here are two reasons why we should accommodate those who are weaker in faith:

1. **To avoid unnecessary conflict.** Those who are weaker in faith often lean toward judgmental attitudes, and there's no need to give them more ammunition.

2. **To protect their faith.** Those who are weaker in faith could stumble because of our freedom. We are called not to boast of our liberty but to live in it with humility.

It's easy to feel like a hypocrite when overly religious people enter the room. Paul was trying to teach us to focus on far more important matters—specifically, how we love. Loving God and loving each other is the issue at hand.

When raising our kids, we had to help them understand this balance. We taught them that there are always going to be people navigating their spiritual lives with inconsistent hardline do's and don'ts. Many will take hard stances on things that God wasn't even clear about. This principle helped us teach them, especially as pastor's kids, why we don't have to live by every "law" that others live by.

RELATE

If we aren't careful, we can fall into sin by condemning others. Turn to God.

Peter's vision on the rooftop in Acts 10 gives us insight into this. God was teaching him that the New Covenant had changed things. The blood of Christ had set him free from the law of sin and death. In Peter's vision, God commanded him to eat what was once forbidden—four-footed animals, reptiles, and birds:

> *"Surely not, Lord!" Peter replied. "I have never eaten anything impure or unclean." The voice spoke to him a second time, "Do not call anything impure that God has made clean."* – Acts 10:14-15 NIV

Paul later recorded another instance where Peter had a "weak in conscience" moment. For a long time, Peter freely ate and fellowshipped with Gentile Christians, who had not been circumcised under Old Covenant law. These believers were accepted by God without undergoing circumcision. But when Jewish believers from James's group arrived—who still clung to the Old Covenant—Peter caved to their pressure:

CHAPTER 7 - TURN FROM YOUR SIN TO GOD

"...he (Peter) began to draw back and separate himself from the Gentiles because he was afraid of those who belonged to the circumcision group. The other Jews joined him in his hypocrisy, so that by their hypocrisy even Barnabas was led astray."
– Galatians 2:12-13 NIV

Look at the outcome—*"Barnabas was led astray."* Even a strong leader like Barnabas was easily persuaded! This is how divisive legalism can become in the church. It spreads quickly, turning small issues into full-blown conflicts.

Peter and James's group started judging, then Barnabas got involved, and soon Paul had to step in and rebuke Peter in front of everyone. Paul put a stop to it—just as he had to do in other churches where legalistic mindsets were creeping in.

Paul's message is loud and clear: It's time for the church to rise and focus on greater things than nitpicking over personal convictions. The blood of Jesus is not fragile. God is not easily offended.

Jesus didn't spill just a few drops of blood—He poured it out completely, lavishly covering our sin. From the Cross, He made a bold declaration: Your sin is no longer the problem. Your lack of love is now the issue.

God Calls Us to Be Experts in Love, Not Sin

Instead of becoming experts in the knowledge of sin, God calls us to excel in love.

If you know your brother is struggling with an addiction, are you going to freely participate in something that might confuse him or tempt him to fall back into it?

Live in your freedom without causing others to stumble.

> *"Therefore, brothers and sisters, since we have confidence to enter the Most Holy Place by the blood of Jesus, by a new and living way opened for us through the curtain, that is, his body, and since we have a great priest over the house of God, let us draw near to God with a sincere heart and with the full assurance that faith brings, having our hearts sprinkled to cleanse us*

from a guilty conscience and having our bodies washed with pure water. Let us hold unswervingly to the hope we profess, for he who promised is faithful. And let us consider how we may spur one another on toward love and good deeds, not giving up meeting together, as some are in the habit of doing, but encouraging one another—and all the more as you see the Day approaching." – Hebrews 10:19-25 NIV

It's time to turn from sin—to turn from legalism, judgment, and the old way of thinking—and turn fully to God's way: LOVE.

Sin Dissipates When We Love

"Above all, love each other deeply, because love covers over a multitude of sins." – 1 Peter 4:8 NIV

It's significant that Peter wrote this passage—considering he was the one Paul had to publicly correct. Peter learned. You are going to fail along the way, but the key is to never stop trying. Keep going back, make things right, and continue practicing the way of love every day.

This is your first duty to Jesus. More than trying to stop sinning—your calling is to start loving. Haven't you tried to stop sinning? Has it worked? Try loving instead.

Turn From Your Sin

Now that you've listed your threats and identified your sin, it's time to turn to God. Jesus said that all of heaven rejoices when one sinner turns to God (Luke 15:7). You may think talking to God about your sin will be terrifying, but it's the opposite—God is gracious and kind. He is eager to help.

God is happy to listen to you talk about your failures and sin! Instead of bringing everyone else's faults before Him, asking Him to change them, bring Him your part. Imagine how God feels when one of His children stops talking about everyone else's shortcomings and starts taking responsibility for their own. Don't you think He leans in a little closer, listening with great pleasure? Scripture tells us God gives grace to the humble—but He resists the proud like a stallion digging in its heels (James 4:6).

"If we say we have no sin, we deceive ourselves, and the

> *truth is not in us. If we confess our sins, He is faithful and just to forgive us our sins and to cleanse us from all unrighteousness. If we say we have not sinned, we make Him out to be a liar, and His word is not in us."*
> – 1 John 1:8-10 ESV

When we confess our sin to Him, it's helpful to recognize the greater sin—not just the wrong we committed, but the lack of love we failed to show. God's command is love.

Meditating on this core value is critical. Learning the way of true love will give you great wisdom. The goal is to strengthen the mental pathways that connect your values with your decision-making so that responding in love becomes second nature. As the Psalmist wrote:

> *"Oh, how I love your law! I meditate on it all day long."*
> – Psalm 119:97 NIV

He was preparing for moments of threat, training his mind in advance to react with love rather than impulse.

Turning to God means living as He lives and loving as He loves. The more time you spend with Him, the more you become like Him—and the less threatening you are to others. Consider this truth:

> *"God's Spirit makes us loving, happy, peaceful, patient, kind, good, faithful, gentle, and self-controlled. There is no law against behaving in any of these ways."*
> – Galatians 5:22-23 CEV

If I had a friend who was loving, happy, peaceful, patient, kind, good, faithful, gentle, and self-controlled, I'd be a fool to push them away! Only an evil society would condemn someone for embodying these virtues. But that's exactly what happened to Jesus.

Living this way doesn't happen by accident. It requires intention. No one naturally embodies these qualities without effort. The flesh is too strong, too self-serving. Only with God's help can we become who He created us to be.

CHAPTER 7 - TURN FROM YOUR SIN TO GOD

**You Do Not Have the Right to Sin,
But You Have the Right to Love**

You do not have the right to do anything that destroys people or relationships—no matter how much you believe you deserve it, or how natural it feels. There is no way to justify it. If your actions hurt others, turn from them and turn to God.

If you're the person who constantly stirs things up in your family, then you're the one hurting and threatening those around you. That's not innocent—it's destructive. Turn. Stop.

Better yet—start. Start loving. Don't just stop sinning—start doing the things the people in your life need and want. You'll be amazed at how quickly your relationships can transform when you stop threatening others with your actions and reactions.

You do have the right to love. We hear it all the time—people insisting others love them "just the way they are." Some people intentionally seek ways to provoke their parents, family, or even society, just to test if they'll still be loved unconditionally. But God's agenda for your life is not for you to go out and be loved—it is for you to go out and love others.

Your love for others should compel you to remove the threats you pose to them. For some, this realization is life-changing.

And remember, the results are up to them. Their love and acceptance of you is their choice.

We see people marching in the streets, demanding love and respect—yet often failing to give love and respect in return. The question is not whether the world will love you, but whether you will love the world as Jesus did.

God Is Looking for a Bride, Not a One-Night Stand

How would you best describe your current relationship with God? Or better yet—how would He describe it?

Throughout Scripture, we see people at various levels in their relationship with Him. Some, like most of the Israelites, had only heard about Him. Jacob wrestled with Him and walked away leaning on Him for the rest of his life. Moses was called God's friend. David had extreme highs and lows with Him. Jeremiah felt the weight of God's sorrow. The disciples walked daily with Jesus—but it was John who came closest to the kind

CHAPTER 7 - TURN FROM YOUR SIN TO GOD

of relationship God desires.

John is called "The Beloved." In his Gospel, whenever he refers to himself, he doesn't use his name—he calls himself "the disciple whom Jesus loved" (John 13:23, 19:26, 20:2, 21:7, 21:20). Jesus never corrected him for this. He never told the other disciples, "Hey, I love you all equally." The truth is, Jesus did love John in a unique way—because each of us is uniquely loved by Him. Like a parent who loves their children differently but fully, God's love for us is incomparable.

Beyond that, John allowed Jesus to love him more. Why? Because John believed Jesus loved him.

Have you ever loved someone who wouldn't let you love them?

When my kids were young, I would ask them every night, "Do you know what I like about you?" They would respond, "Every single day." I started this to remind them that they were a highlight of my day.

But one of my kids struggled with believing they were loved.

Even as a toddler, they remembered discipline more than affection. If I played with the other kids, they felt rejected—even if I had just spent time with them. Their constant need for validation became overwhelming. After addressing it, I told them, "Let's change what I say at bedtime. From now on, when I ask, 'Do you know what I like about you?' you'll say, 'I know you love me.'" We did this for years.

And it helped tremendously.

Now, I can freely show this child love. The love blocker was removed.

Understanding Our Relationship with God

The Bible presents several ways God relates to us, each offering a different perspective of His deep connection with us:

- He calls us His children (1 John 3:1).

- We are His bride, as part of the Body of Christ—the church (John 3:29; 2 Corinthians 11:2).

CHAPTER 7 - TURN FROM YOUR SIN TO GOD

- We are His business partners, entrusted with His work on earth (1 Corinthians 3:9).

In all these relationships, God is waiting for us to believe He loves us. Like a good father, He operates with the long-term health of His child in mind. He wants us to grow up, mature, and be healthy—not constantly question His love just because He didn't answer a prayer the way we wanted.

Imagine being married to someone who never believes you love them, no matter what you do. A relationship like that is exhausting and unproductive. If both partners are stuck in an endless loop of trying to prove love, they'll never accomplish anything meaningful together. There won't be energy for raising healthy kids, building a life, or serving a community. Jealousy and manipulation will begin to suffocate the relationship.

God wants you to believe He loves you. And when you do, it frees Him to love you even more! He won't engage in business with those who don't trust Him. If you want to partner with God in life, let Him love you—believe in His love.

RELATE

Hard Times Are Opportunities to Love God

Instead of seeing difficult times as proof that God doesn't love us, what if we saw them as our opportunity to love Him?

Without hard times, when would we truly express love to God? The entire book of Job is about proving that Job truly loved God—not about whether God loved Job. Job's suffering was allowed because Satan challenged his love, claiming that Job only served God because of His blessings. Every loss and painful moment gave Job a chance to turn away—but he never did. Job's story wasn't about God's love for Job; it was about Job's love for God.

Paul and Silas sang worship songs in a prison cell. That's what love looks like (Acts 16:16ff).

Your trials are your opportunity to show love to God. He's looking for a bride—someone committed, faithful, and willing to love Him through it all.

God desires more than religious ceremonies and traditions. He even desires more than a relationship—He wants love. A love so real that it changes how we live. A love that others can see as we walk in humility, patience, generosity, gratitude, and contentment.

Jesus said:

> *"By this everyone will know that you are my disciples, if you love one another."* – John 13:35 NIV

Turn to God. Love Him by loving others.

Make Things Right

When we understand that sin is a love issue, simply confessing it to God in secret isn't enough. That's often all modern church culture tells us to do—confess it privately and move on.

But many believers still walk away feeling like something is missing. That's because something is missing. The secret to stepping into real love is making things right when you have done wrong.

When was the last time you heard of someone who gossiped about a friend going back to apologize and make it right?

Churches are full of people who are afraid to make things right because it would mean admitting they were wrong. But isn't that exactly what Jesus called us to do?

So instead, we fake it. We show up at church, lift our hands in worship, and act like we have it all together. Visitors walk in and think they're the only ones struggling, while longtime church members know about all the unresolved conflict brewing beneath the surface.

Should we keep worshiping together even when there's unresolved tension? Absolutely!

But... Jesus' people must also start making things right with one another.

Learning to Be Wrong

When I started practicing RELATE, I was ashamed of my history as a Christian. I had spent years working hard to look good to others. I thought my job as a pastor was to appear perfect—perfect wife, perfect kids, perfect sermons, perfect lawn, perfect car. When I couldn't be perfect, I had to make sure I at least looked perfect.

Which meant… I lived a lie.

Worse, I could never admit when I was wrong. I always had an excuse. "I didn't mean it that way." "I have a good heart." "I was just trying to help." I was too afraid of looking weak. And people knew it.

Then, I met George.

George was an unfiltered, straight-talking, no-nonsense kind of guy. He wasn't into appearances, didn't care about fashion, and had no fear of germs. He often showed up to church in an ice-cream-stained t-shirt, shorts, tall white socks, and work boots.

Before coming to Christ, George had wrecked his life. He had spent years making bad choices. He did jail time for it. Alcohol was his struggle, but before he passed away, he had been sober for 30 years and had helped hundreds of others stay clean.

Because of his past, he spent the rest of his life working to make things right with his children, family, and community.

RELATE

George gave me permission to be wrong.

He was the first person I could confess my mistakes to—without fear. He still respected me, still listened to my sermons, and still believed in me.

I finally understood that God could love me that way too.

Once I started applying RELATE, I realized I hadn't been honest with people. I had failed to set boundaries and let some relationships drain me instead of being healthy.

Making things right wasn't just about apologizing—it was also about teaching people how to treat me.

Making things right is also a great motivator to stop sinning in the first place.

- If you stole something—return it.

- If you lied about someone—tell the truth.

- If you slandered a friend—apologize and clear their name.

- If you used sin to cope with your fears, and it hurt others—make amends.

- If you haven't cleaned up the mess you made, you now know what's missing in your relationship with God.

Jesus said:

"You're familiar with the command to the ancients, 'Do not murder.' I'm telling you that anyone who is so much as angry with a brother or sister is guilty of murder. Carelessly call a brother 'idiot!' and you just might find yourself hauled into court. Thoughtlessly yell 'stupid!' at a sister and you are on the brink of hellfire. The simple moral fact is that words kill. This is how I want you to conduct yourself in these matters. If you enter your place of worship and, about to make an offering, you suddenly remember a grudge a friend has against you, abandon your offering, leave immediately, go to this friend and make things right. Then and only then, come back and work things out with God. Or say you're out on the street and an old enemy accosts you. Don't

RELATE

lose a minute. Make the first move; make things right with him." – Matthew 5:21-25 MSG

<< ACTION >>

Pray. Talk to God about your part. Confess your sin. Ask for wisdom on how to go back and make things right where possible.

<< QUESTIONS TO REFLECT ON >>

- In what ways have you been tempted to focus on other people's sins instead of your own?

- How do you typically respond when you realize you've done something wrong? Do you confess it, ignore it, or try to justify it?

- Have you ever confessed your sin to God but avoided making things right with the person you hurt? What's holding you back?

CHAPTER 7 - TURN FROM YOUR SIN TO GOD

- How would your relationship with God change if you believed He delights in your repentance rather than being disappointed in you?

- Have you ever believed the lie that being wrong makes you weak? How does this belief impact your relationships?

- Who in your life has given you permission to be wrong and still feel loved? How can you offer that same grace to others?

- What practical steps can you take this week to make things right with someone you've hurt?

- How might your relationships change if you prioritized love over the need to be right?

CHAPTER 8

"E" Enlist Accountability

Whether it was a parable Jesus told or a real-life story, the Bible is full of examples of people who could have used a true friend to hold them accountable. What if Moses had rerouted his thinking before striking the rock and talked to someone who could calm him down (Numbers 20)? What if King David had reached out to a friend instead of calling Bathsheba over to the palace (2 Samuel 11)? Or when Ananias and Sapphira decided to take a shortcut to being respected in the church by lying to Peter about how much money they were giving—what if they had called a friend (Acts 5)?

The biggest failures in your life are often so easy to see—by someone else. Pride is deceiving; it makes anger, lust, greed, gluttony, envy, and sloth seem rational, even permissible. We are blind to our own self-sabotaging plans. When our flesh is at work, we need help to see.

Enlisting accountability is essential to the RELATE process because it challenges you to:

1. Recognize your threats and where you lack trust in God.
2. Acknowledge your part in the sin you are participating in.
3. Take responsibility and make things right when you have wronged someone.

If I'm surrounded by people who never challenge me, that's a problem. If my friends always support my offenses, never push me to trust God, and never remind me of my values, then I need new friends.

This is one of the reasons many well-known celebrities died young. Tragically, the people around them were dependent on their talent for their own security. Their inner circles benefited from their success, which meant challenging them could result in losing access, status, or financial stability. If you were part of Elvis's close circle, telling him to stop taking drugs might have meant losing your livelihood—so no one did.

It's important to understand that the people in your life may find their own sense of security, social status, or intimacy through their relationship with you. If you make it clear that honesty is unwelcome, and it's not safe for them to challenge you, you create a zero-accountability environment. And without accountability, there is no lasting success.

You and I both need people in our lives who care more about our eternal well-being than whether we like them. That is real love.

This is what the church is meant to provide—a safe place where people can practice love, fail, make things right, and try again. But it has to start with you.

CHAPTER 8 - ENLIST ACCOUNTABILITY

You need people who, when your emotions are running high, will ask, "How are you being threatened?" It's easy to find people who will jump on board with you and say, "Yeah, your boss is a jerk!" or "Your husband was totally wrong to say that!" But there's no power in a victim mindset. Even if you're mostly right, your job is to identify where you are wrong and take responsibility for it.

Solomon wrote, "Wounds from a friend can be trusted, but an enemy multiplies kisses." – Proverbs 27:6 NIV

A fool with many friends is a man loved by none. But a fool with no friends is a man loved by many. In other words, a fool who ends up alone was actually loved enough by those around him to be told the truth—so much so that they refused to enable his choices. Real friends don't support you in your foolishness. They love you enough to tell you the truth, even if it means you walk away.

RELATE

Accountability to Spot Your Threats

When someone does something that threatens us, our instinctive reaction is to say, "They threatened me." But if you reroute your thinking, you can shift that perspective to, "I took that as a threat." There's a big difference between those two statements. One keeps you in victim mode, blaming others for how you feel. The other allows you to own it—and helps you take responsibility for your response. Even if someone intended to threaten you, you still have control over how you process it.

But sometimes, it's hard to spot how we are threatened. We need help. Others can often see in us what we cannot see in ourselves. And God will often use people in our lives to reveal insights we might never recognize on our own.

King David wrote, "But who can discern their own errors?" – Psalm 19:12 NIV

It's far easier to see how others are threatened than to recognize our own threats. When we step back and ask God to help us see the struggles in someone else, it's often obvious. But when it comes to our own blind spots, we need trusted people to help us uncover them.

A good accountability partner will help you recognize the things you *say* don't matter, but, actually *do*—like your social status. In Christian circles, caring about how we appear to others is often looked at as being shallow or unspiritual. So we deny it.

We pretend it's not important. But it is important—because it affects our decisions, our relationships, and even our witness. A true friend will help you see reality.

Pride convinces us that we are self-sufficient and unaffected by anything. Humility allows us to acknowledge our struggles, confess our threats to God and others, and find freedom. When we do that, those threats lose their power.

RELATE

Accountability to See Your Part

Just as accountability helps us spot our threats, it also helps us recognize where we are responsible. When you allow someone else to walk with you in this process, God will often use them to reveal hidden areas of sin.

Our pride works against us, convincing us that we're right, innocent, or justified. It is not natural for us to admit when we're wrong. In fact, without outside help, we rarely do.

One of the beautiful things about RELATE is that confession doesn't require deep dives into every detail. Sometimes, simply saying, "I've been struggling with pride and lust," is enough.

Oversharing can sometimes do more harm than good—giving your accountability partner mental images that are hard to erase. I've also seen situations in which discussing sin too much actually fuels temptation, rather than bringing freedom. What was intended to break sin's hold can, if not handled wisely, turn into a trap that pulls you back in.

CHAPTER 8 - ENLIST ACCOUNTABILITY

That's why accountability must be rooted in love. A true friend who walks with you after confession is a reflection of the Gospel.

As believers, we are commanded to love and restore those who are repentant. No matter what is confessed, we are not permitted to use it against them for our own gain. That's the beauty of God's grace and what makes accountability so powerful.

Not only do you need people who will help you see your part—you must be that person for others. When you are accountable yourself, you are in a better position to walk alongside others in their struggles.

Accountability to Make It Right

My friend George used to share a story that perfectly illustrates the power of accountability. He once mentored a man who, years earlier, had developed a habit of stealing a bag of ice from a local gas station every week. He did this for several years, and though he had long since changed his ways, the guilt still weighed on him. The problem? That store no longer existed. There was no way to go back and repay the exact debt.

George saw the bigger picture and offered him a creative solution: for the next few years, he would go to a different store, pay for a bag of ice—but never take it. Week after week, he did exactly that. It became an exercise in integrity—a way to make things right even when direct restitution wasn't possible.

Having someone to walk through this process with you brings clarity, direction, and accountability. They also serve as a source of encouragement when you take action to repair what was broken. But just as they can help determine how to make things right, they can also help you discern when you don't need to.

Sometimes we carry guilt for things that weren't actually our fault. And in cases where the person we wronged doesn't want to hear from us, a trusted friend can help us find a different way to seek resolution.

CHAPTER 8 - ENLIST ACCOUNTABILITY

A while back, I had to confront someone with an ongoing issue in our relationship. I needed someone outside of me to coach me through the situation; otherwise, there was no hope I'd be able to address it in such a way that there would be room for restoration afterward. I enlisted accountability. He helped me make sure I had removed the plank from my own eye before attempting to address the issue. And when the conversation didn't go well, having someone to debrief with afterward was invaluable.

Even though I had handled the situation with a measure of patience, the person completely dismissed my concerns. They latched onto my frustration, using it as an excuse to ignore what I was saying. That's how people avoid dealing with the truth—if they don't like what you're saying, they'll find a reason to discredit you.

It took over two years of patience and consistency before any real progress was made. My accountability partner kept reminding me that my responsibility wasn't to force the other person to change—it was to do my part. And with time, I was able to take small steps toward making things right. Even though they never reciprocated, I had peace knowing I had done what God called me to do.

If you're serious about going back and making things right, tell someone who will hold you accountable. They'll not only encourage you, but they'll help you walk through it with wisdom.

<< ACTION STEP >>

Ask God to lead you to someone you can trust for accountability. It doesn't need to be a spiritual giant—just someone who is a little ahead of you in their walk with Christ and is willing to walk through RELATE with you.

<< QUESTIONS TO REFLECT ON >>

1. Who in your life is honest enough to tell you the truth, even when you might not want to hear it? Have you given them permission to speak freely into your life?

CHAPTER 8 - ENLIST ACCOUNTABILITY

2. When was the last time someone challenged you about an attitude, behavior, or decision? How did you respond—defensive or receptive?

3. Do the people closest to you encourage you to grow spiritually, or enable you to stay stuck? Are you surrounding yourself with people who always agree with you, or with people who care more about your character than your comfort?

4. Think about a time when you were blind to your own mistakes. How might accountability have helped you avoid that situation?

5. What threats in your life are hardest for you to see clearly? Who do you trust to help you spot those threats?

6. Have you ever confessed something difficult to an accountability partner? What was the outcome? How did it affect your freedom and growth?

7. Is there a situation right now where you need to make

something right, but you haven't? Who can you ask to help you walk through that process?

8. Are you the kind of friend who will lovingly tell the truth and hold others accountable? How can you grow in that role?

9. Have you ever been tempted to use someone's confession against them? How can you guard your heart and stay committed to grace and restoration?

10. What step will you take this week to enlist accountability in your life? Write down one person you will ask to be an accountability partner.

CHAPTER 9

Doing Relationships God's Way

God Lives Like This Even When No One Else Does

If this were an easy road, everyone would already be walking it. The reality is, relationships take work—but that work brings reward. And this kind of work yields results that last a lifetime. Even if you're the only one putting in the effort, it will pay great dividends. God Himself is banking on it. That alone should tell you something. If God told you to invest all your money in a certain stock, you'd be ecstatic! In the same way, He calls you to invest your entire life in doing relationships His way—and He leads by example.

RELATE is the invitation and the path to fulfilling your role in relationships, regardless of what others choose to do. When all is said and done, you will stand before God, accountable for how you conducted yourself with the people He loves so dearly.

God calls you to do relationships as He does. That's one of the greatest benefits of having the Bible—it teaches us His ways. Here are some key relational behaviors from Scripture that show us how God Himself relates to us.

How Does God Do Relationships?

1. God sets His affections on every individual.

Jesus spoke about how deeply God sees and knows each of us. He has counted every hair on your head (Luke 12:7). He doesn't use or manipulate people. He loves and blesses those who welcome Him into relationship.

Consider the doctrine of Mary's immaculate conception. We often assume it's because God wanted us to know she was pure and that Jesus was her first child. But what if there was something even more profound at play? What if God was declaring to the world: *I did not use or abuse Mary. I placed My seed within her without harm or selfish gain.* This sets Him apart from the womanizing "sons of God" mentioned in the Old Testament. God's love is pure and protective.

God is possessive of you in the best way. He sees everything you are going through, and one day He will make all things right. He will wipe away your tears and reward you for the love you've shown in this life. Until then, He calls you to trust Him and reflect His love to others.

You belong to Him.

If you curse Him because of your life's pain, you'll miss out on all He has for you. But if you trust Him through your pain, you won't miss out on anything.

God is so vast that He can love every single one of us deeply and personally. And the more you believe He loves you, the more you will experience His love. The more you believe He loves those around you, the more you will be able to love them too.

And this is just as true: How you treat others matters deeply to Him. Even if they don't love or believe in Him, they still belong to Him.

Loving His Way is Living Without Fear and Without Restraint

One day, after a terrorist attack in America dominated the news, I was in a local business when a Muslim that worked there—who knew I was a Christian pastor—signaled for me to follow him. Without a word, we got on an elevator, rode it down to the basement, and walked down a quiet corridor. He seemed nervous, constantly glancing around to ensure no one was watching. I'll admit, I started to feel uneasy too.

When we arrived at a break area with a TV broadcasting the news, he finally spoke. "I need to know what you think of me."

I was taken aback. "I don't understand. Please clarify."

He looked at me with deep concern. "This terrorist attack today. Do you want to kill my wife, my kids, and me?"

His question stunned me. "Oh goodness, no," I said. "In fact, my God demands that I be willing to lay down my life for you and your family."

His expression shifted from fear to disbelief. He had never heard that before.

"Where did you get the idea that I would want to harm you?" I asked.

"That's what we've been told by our religious leaders," he admitted.

In that moment, I realized how deeply distorted perceptions of Christianity can be. The God of the Bible—the One we serve—loves every single person. And He calls us to live without fear and to love without restraint. Our faith isn't just about how we treat God; it's about how we treat others, especially those who don't share our beliefs.

2. God invites us to enter a covenant with Him.

God doesn't extend a casual invitation—He calls us into a covenant. He isn't looking for a date; He's looking for a bride.

About a year and a half after becoming a widower, I went on a handful of dates, and the experience gave me a new perspective. I had been married for almost 29 years and with her for 30. Marriage is what I knew—it's what I wanted. So, I was looking for a bride, not just a date.

With each date, I could usually tell within the first minute whether a connection was possible. Technology filters out the basics—whether she's a Christian, has kids, or owns a cat—but the real test comes in person.

I considered things like: *Did she try to make a good first impression? Did she put effort into her appearance?* While outward appearance isn't everything, I appreciate someone who presents herself well.

I also paid attention to whether my date was a good listener. Was she interested in what I had to say, or did she immediately start talking the moment we sat down and keep going for 45 minutes straight?

And then, I noticed whether she knew what she liked and didn't like. I wasn't interested in someone with no desire, no direction, and no passion for anything. Someone who knows who they are and what they want is far more appealing than someone who doesn't.

Thankfully, God knew the woman I would be perfectly suited for and who would be exactly what I wanted in a mate. When I met my wife, Amy, we felt a strong connection immediately. Our first date lasted about five hours, and we are happily married today! Amazingly, she has 2 cats—something I thought was a dealbreaker. But she accommodates for me, my allergies and needs, and we have built a beautiful home full of laughter and love together. That's relationship. That's love.

I hope you understand there's a bit of humor in all this, but the truth is, God is looking for the same intentionality in us. He's not searching for passive followers, but for a bride devoted to knowing Him.

> *"There's a private place reserved for the devoted lovers of Yahweh, where they sit near him and receive the revelation-secrets of his promises." – Psalm 25:14 TPT*

God desires to have a relationship with you, and as you

commit yourself more and more to Him, He shares more and more secrets about Himself with you.

Jesus illustrated this in His parable of the ten virgins in Matthew 25:1–13. Five of the women prepared themselves with extra oil, anticipating delays. The other five were careless—unprepared when the bridegroom arrived. When they realized their mistake, they begged for help—but it was too late.

They had time. They had the opportunity. But they didn't care enough to prepare themselves for Him.

Think about that. God is interested in a deep, personal relationship with you, and He used a story about a groom and brides to make the point. God desires intimacy. He's not just looking for people who knock on the door at the last minute. He's calling those who pursue Him passionately, who anticipate His return, and who take extra measures to be ready. The five unprepared brides banged on the door—but where was their passion before that moment?

CHAPTER 9 - DOING RELATIONSHIPS GOD'S WAY

Don't Make Cheap Invitations in Your Life—Make Covenants

While on vacation, I decided to try something different and attended an amateur stand-up comedy night at a local club. I love stand-up and laughter, so I was curious about the experience. I didn't know what to expect.

Each comedian had about five minutes to showcase their best material, hoping to make people laugh. But what I witnessed wasn't comedy—it was a desperate attempt to normalize pain. Their humor wasn't uplifting; it reflected their suffering, thinly masked by laughter.

It was an eye-opening experience, especially when compared to the environment of my church family.

The church is so different from the world. At least mine is. God's house provides deep, loving, caring, committed relationships. We don't get up and laugh about being in pain. We don't celebrate drug use, sexual confusion, or depression. Instead, we worship a living God who sings over us! We speak of His goodness, His purpose, His love—and we encourage each other with hope and inspiration.

The world may call us judgmental prudes—using more colorful language—but they have no idea what they're settling for in comparison to the abundant life in Christ.

God, help them to see what they're missing!

3. God clearly teaches what He likes and doesn't like.

Imagine how devastating it would be to stand before God after death and realize you were supposed to guess what He liked and didn't like during your life. Many people are frustrated with God because of His boundaries—but what about appreciating Him for making them clear?

God's guidelines aren't about control; they're about love. When you truly love someone, you accommodate for them. It's one thing to love someone enough to die for them, but what about *living* for them? If you love God, you will live for Him—striving to do your best in every way?

Yes, as humans, we will inevitably fail at times, but thank God for His unwavering love. He has promised never to leave us or forsake us. The real question is: Will we leave or forsake Him?

At its core, all of God's commands are about love—loving Him and loving others.

- Love God.
- Love people.
- Do no harm.
- Do not use others for your own pleasure.
- Do not abuse or abandon.
- Do not live a life of selfishness and fear.
- Instead, live a life of love, devotion, commitment, protection, and giving.

While the world insists on the right to "be me," constantly reinventing and redefining itself, God patiently waits for us to abandon ourselves and live for Him, so we can discover our true identity—the one He purposefully designed. It's interesting that those who claim they are just trying to "be themselves" are often the ones continually trying to change who they are. But what if true peace comes from accepting God's design? What if, instead of trying to fit into an image of what the world says is ideal, we looked in the mirror and simply embraced what He created?

God's likes and dislikes are perfectly aligned with who you truly are—the person He intentionally created you to be. You don't need to alter your body or identity to find fulfillment. Instead, choose to love God, trust Him and accept yourself as He sees you.

After all—God desires to dwell within you, to make His home in you.

> *"This kingdom of faith is now your home country. You're no longer strangers or outsiders. You belong here, with as much right to the name Christian as anyone. God is building a home."* – Eph. 2:19-22 MSG

He is not looking for an occasional date—someone who visits Him only on Sunday mornings once or twice a month. Or worse, only on Christmas and Easter. He isn't interested a half-hearted relationship.

That's something worth reflecting on if you consider yourself a CEO—Christmas and Easter Only. Those who only "date" God on holidays know little more than the basics: He was born, He died, and He rose again. But there is so much more to God!

Teach Others What You Like and Don't Like

Give others the opportunity to know and love you. Be honest with them. Help them understand your boundaries. If they truly want to love you, they will respect the boundaries you set. And likewise, be willing to do the same for them.

When I do premarital counseling, one of the key questions I ask is:

"What could your spouse do that would warrant a divorce?"

This is one of the most important questions couples should answer before getting married. Boundaries matter. Knowing what is non-negotiable in a relationship is crucial to keeping it intact.

But daily life in relationships is much more nuanced.

Staying married isn't just about sexual fidelity—it's about

living together in love, joy, peace, patience, kindness, goodness, faithfulness, gentleness, and self-control. It's about the whole package.

When you stop communicating what you like and don't like in a relationship, you are giving up on that person truly loving you, and that relationship is heading toward a dead-end.

Thankfully, God has clearly communicated His boundaries because He loves you and wants to deeply connected to you!

4. God invites us to do what He does.

> *"He creates each of us by Christ Jesus to join him in the work he does, the good work he has gotten ready for us to do, work we had better be doing." –* Eph. 2:10 MSG

The God of the universe extends an invitation to *us* to participate in *His* mission.

There's no greater validation of trust than being invited to join someone in the work they care most about. That's exactly what God does for us. And honestly, it's hard to comprehend.

Why would the Creator of all things choose to include us? The truth is, we don't need to fully understand why God wants us. We just need to embrace the fact that He does.

God calls His work with humanity His inheritance. We are His portion—His delight. And His invitation to join in that work is no small thing.

Jesus affirmed this calling when He gave the Great Commission:

> *Then Jesus came to them and said, "All authority in heaven and on earth has been given to me. Therefore go and make disciples of all nations, baptizing them in the name of the Father and of the Son and of the Holy Spirit, and teaching them to obey everything I have commanded you. And surely I am with you always, to the very end of the age." – Matthew 28:18-20 NIV*

Whatever you love—cooking, hiking, cars, fishing—invite others to share in it. But remember, true intimacy requires more than just shared hobbies or recreation. Ask yourself: Are you building something meaningful with someone?

This is the beauty of the church! God gave us something to build together.

1 Corinthians 12 paints a powerful picture of God's people working as one body—each of us playing our part.

So invite others to join you in a meaningful life with Christ!

5. God invites us to intimacy.

Jesus made Himself completely vulnerable to humanity. He came as a baby—nursing at His mother's breast. The Creator of the universe needed to be fed, coddled, protected, and held by His own creation. Imagine that. God, in His infinite power, humbled Himself to such a degree that He relied on human hands to care for Him.

Throughout history, the Bible has been the most profound and inspiring book ever written. It has influenced more songs, poems, paintings, films, and literature—and transformed more lives—than perhaps all other books combined. And yet, it's more than a historical document. It's God's love letter to you. He invites you to read it, explore its depths, and truly know

Him.

Beyond that, God has made it possible—through the death, burial, resurrection, and ascension of Jesus—for His Spirit to not only live inside you but also rest upon you. In Acts 2, the baptism in the Holy Spirit is revealed as a deeply personal and intimate encounter with Christ's Spirit.

God wants to be closer to you.

Sadly, this sacred experience has often been misrepresented—used as a display of power or spiritual superiority—leaving many confused or hesitant. But this intimate gift was never meant to be a spectacle. While the gift of tongues with interpretation has great value for edifying the church body, God's primary intention is deeply personal: to allow His Spirit to pray from within you, to strengthen you, and to help you experience His presence in a tangible way.

Invite People to Intimacy

One of the hardest things in life is opening yourself up to someone. But even harder is becoming the kind of person others feel safe opening up to. Intimacy is about someone genuinely trusting you with their deepest thoughts, struggles, and hopes.

Why is intimacy in friendships—and even in marriage—so difficult? Much of it comes down to our inability to teach one another how to be closer, safer, and more trustworthy.

If you want intimacy, let people share their hearts without immediately trying to fix them—unless they ask you to. When someone trusts you enough to be vulnerable, don't judge them or reach for your "toolbox" to prove how wise you are. Just listen.

Another tip: *stop hijacking conversations*. Set aside your own struggles and past pain—and truly listen to theirs. If I say, "I've got bad allergies today," don't let your first response be, "Oh yes, mine are awful!" If you do, that may be as deep as the relationship ever goes.

A call to intimacy means giving people a safe space to be real. If you weaponize their words or cause them more pain, they won't trust you at that level again.

Be willing to be vulnerable. And when someone trusts you with their heart—honor that trust.

6. God chooses to have a relationship with those who honor Him.

Another way to say it is this: God will never force Himself on someone who does not honor, respect, or draw close to Him. But for those who seek Him—He is theirs.

God will never impose a relationship on you. You are free to choose Him—or not. But know this: it's personal to Him. He has made it abundantly clear that He is a jealous God (Exodus 20:5).

Jealousy is the deep longing to be chosen—to be loved above all else. God knows how good He will be to you, and when you choose to worship something else—whether it be success, people, or worldly pleasures—He feels it. And yet, He will never force you into heaven. Instead, He lovingly pursues you, warning you of the consequences of rejecting Him.

Jesus, with both love and solemn warning, said:

> *"Do not be afraid of those who kill the body but cannot kill the soul. Rather, be afraid of the One who can destroy both soul and body in hell. Are not two sparrows sold for a penny? Yet not one of them will fall to the ground outside your Father's care. And even the very hairs of your head are all numbered. So don't be afraid; you are worth more than many sparrows."*
>
> – Matthew 10:28–31 NIV

God wants you—but He will not force you. Will you choose Him?

Let People Choose You

God chooses to have a relationship with those who honor, respect, and draw close to Him. He doesn't force Himself on anyone—and neither should you.

Don't chase people down or try to force relationships, no matter how much you want them. Even in marriage, where vows have been exchanged, each person must continually choose the relationship. Embracing that truth keeps both partners accountable to be their best selves.

And sometimes, you simply have to let people go.

If someone has better things to do—or would rather be alone—let them go. If they want to believe bad things about you, let them. The sooner, the better.

7. God removed the "threat" He is to us.

When Jesus stretched out His arms on the cross, He was declaring: *I am not a threat to you.*

He could have come riding on the clouds in full battle mode. Instead, He came as a baby. When He rode into Jerusalem on Palm Sunday, He could have arrived on a majestic stallion, showing His power and declaring His kingship. Instead, He came gently—dragging His feet on a young donkey.

Jesus intentionally removed the threats He posed to others. His goal was to love and bring people into relationship with Him.

RELATE

Remove the Threats You Pose to Others

As we learned in Chapter 5, *List Your Threats*, everyone is managing three core threats in life: Security, Significance, and Intimate Relationships. You can't control how others perceive you, but you can be intentional about not being a threat.

Ask yourself:

- Am I a threat to my spouse or kids?

- Am I a threat to my boss or coworkers? What could I do differently to help them feel safe with me?

- Am I a threat to people driving around me on the road?

If your life is causing harm or instability to others, it's time to RELATE. Because God has removed any threat—through His grace, so can we.

8. God doesn't present Himself as perfect—He allows you to draw your own conclusions.

God doesn't force you to see Him in a particular way. He allows you to form your own thoughts about Him.

Whatever objections you have—whether about suffering, injustice, or the brokenness of the world—if you choose to draw close to Him and trust Him, He will help you understand. He will share His secrets with you.

But for those who choose to dismiss Him as a heartless Almighty, indifferent to murder, suffering, disease, and all the world's evils—He allows them to believe that. He does not force His love on anyone.

Yet here's a truth about loving others: *You cannot love someone only if they're perfect.* Love only happens when you choose to look past imperfections.

You don't know how much love exists in any relationship until it's tested—by struggle and even failure. Your spouse doesn't know how much you love them until they see you do something no one else would do for them.

I had no idea that, in the last six months of her life, I would be cleaning and changing my wife's colostomy bag multiple times a day. But I did. And I wouldn't trade those moments by her bedside for anything. It was the proof that I loved her—not just for her beauty, but for who she was. What a privilege.

This isn't an exhaustive list of God's ways in relationships. But these are qualities that—if you embrace them—will transform how you live out RELATE.

Drop the Facade of Perfection

Before I started living out RELATE, as a pastor, I failed miserably at this one. I was obsessed with managing how others perceived me. I couldn't imagine standing in the pulpit and being taken seriously if people knew I wasn't perfect.

And now? I don't worry about it or let insecurity hold me back. In fact, I can now laugh at my faults and easily share my shortcomings. I'm just a guy…a foolish one at that. People can judge or believe what they want about me.

I drive a Camaro—a nice one. I enjoy banter, jokes, and laughter. I once (maybe twice) ate an entire box of Tastykake Bells while taking a drive in my car. I'm not perfect. In fact, consider this: Jesus died on a cross because that's how much I needed saving. And I know it.

This isn't a roundabout way of trying to sound humble. I'm simply able to be honest about myself now, because I know what I'm like in my own strength—and who I truly am in God's sight.

RELATE is a path to a full and free life, but it requires effort, discipline, and focus to get there.

Relationship Is Tangible—In a Different Way

How do you know if you have a real relationship with God? The same way you know if you have a good marriage:

- **Is there intimacy?** Do you draw close to Him? Does He share His secrets with you?

- **Is there accommodation?** Do you adjust your life for Him—choosing His ways over your own?

- **Is there a shared mission?** Have you embraced His work as your own?

RELATE

<< QUESTIONS TO REFLECT ON >>

- In what ways have you been trying to control or force relationships instead of allowing others to choose you?

- What are some specific ways you might be posing a threat to others—whether through your words, actions, or attitudes?

- Are you pretending to have it all together for the approval of others? What would it look like to drop the facade and be honest?

- How would you describe your relationship with God right now? Is there intimacy, accommodation, and a shared mission—or have you settled for something less?

CHAPTER 10

RELATE Changes Things

Marriages restored, jobs saved—and sometimes even promotions granted, parents learning to love better, friendships repaired, addicts freed. These are just a few of the incredible transformations I've witnessed over the years when people apply the RELATE framework. This method isn't just a theory—it's a practical tool that has changed lives in powerful ways.

Let's look at some real-life examples of how RELATE brings lasting change.

Mike's Story: Learning to Listen

Mike called me and wanted to meet—his voice strained with desperation.

We arranged to sit down at an IHOP, and when I arrived, he was already there, hunched over a cup of black coffee, staring at it as if it held the answers he needed. The stress on his face was unmistakable.

"She left," he said, his voice cracking. "I can't live without her."

His hands shook as he clutched his coffee cup, and within moments, tears spilled onto the table. Until that moment, Mike had been completely closed off to outside input. He believed he had life figured out and was in control. His plan was solid, and things were going his way. What he didn't realize was that his wife was done with "his way."

For years, she had tried to share her dreams with Mike, but he never really listened. She objected when he decided they should move out to the country, but he dismissed her concerns, and they moved anyway. She wanted more than one child—it fell on deaf ears.

Then one day, she found her voice. In one short note, she communicated with enough power that Mike finally 'heard' her: *I want a divorce. Don't try to call.*

Mike was brought to his knees—the illusion of control had shattered. Over the next hour and a half in that booth, I walked Mike through RELATE. For the first time, he reflected and considered how awful he had sounded to his wife. He truly understood how he had treated her for years.

What Mike thought she needed to hear was, "I can't live without you." But to her, those words now felt suffocating—even offensive. She no longer saw his neediness as love; she saw it as selfishness.

Through the RELATE process, Mike gained a new perspective and finally understood what he had done wrong. Over the next few weeks, he changed—and she came back home. And come to find out, she didn't really need to move. She just needed a real relationship with her husband. They both changed.

As of this writing, over a decade later, they are still together. Reflecting back, they had no idea how important their reconciliation would be. It was imperative for them to work things out so they could face the challenges of life together—including the loss of their teenage son just a few years later. What if they hadn't?

Sarah's Story: From Chaos to Stability

Sarah was finally clean. She had broken free from drugs after three painful years. But addiction had left her life in shambles, and she was still spiraling.

Being a single parent was overwhelming, and pills had numbed the pain—the loneliness, the feeling of being unwanted, and the buried wounds from her childhood. She had grown up in an abusive home and endured sexual abuse at the hands of family members.

Her downward spiral wasn't just emotional. In the last four months, she had burned through three jobs. She had neglected responsibilities—unpaid parking tickets, no car insurance, and hadn't filed her taxes in years. She was drowning.

Sarah needed a job so she could provide for herself and her daughter. She desperately needed to dig herself out of the hole she was in.

CHAPTER 10 - RELATE CHANGES THINGS

Her most immediate need was to figure out why she kept losing jobs. When I met with her, she was a little rough around the edges. She had a worn and tattered look, with faded pink hair—the last remnants of her past life. But Sarah was ready to listen.

She began telling me her side of the stories about the three jobs she had lost.

As we worked through the RELATE process, Sarah had a breakthrough. For the first time, she realized she was a threat to the people around her.

At every job, she unknowingly intimidated her coworkers. She came in too aggressively, imposing herself too quickly. Without realizing it, she threatened those who had been there longer by pointing out problems before earning their trust. She found skeletons in the closet and exposed them before proving she was part of the team.

Her responsibility, when given another job, would be to go in and not be a threat. To not have answers for every problem. To not act like she deserved a place at the table—but to earn one.

That week, she called to tell me she had landed another job. This time, she took a different approach. Over the next few months, I coached her as she applied RELATE in real time. She's doing great and has kept that job for over three years with outstanding reviews. She now has a higher-paying job, a stable home, and a thriving daughter. She caught up on her taxes, paid off her fines, and has become a vital member of her church.

She even looks like a completely new person! She is healthy, has a bright smile, and a confidence rooted in wisdom.

RELATE changed everything. The difference? She learned to relate to people in a way that built trust instead of fear. God's way of living works.

Sanity vs. Insanity: A Pastor's Story

I received a call one day. One of those calls every pastor dreads. A 16-year-old girl from our community died in a car accident.

On my way to be with her family, my heart was breaking

too. Meeting with parents who have lost a child is devastating. Walking into grief like that is one of the hardest parts of ministry.

After getting through the initial shock and waves of tears, her parents spoke the words I was most fearful to hear: "We want you to do her funeral."

"Of course. Absolutely," I said, wanting to do anything to support them in their time of need. Although, on the inside, I silently prayed, "God, I can't do this! Please, let someone else handle this girl's funeral."

I spent the following week preparing for one of the hardest days in my ministry. It was an enormous responsibility, and the service would live in the family's memory forever.

The funeral was set in a large, formal church, where the girl's grandparents were members. I had never met the church's pastor, but I expected she would be there to support the family and help me.

As I pulled into the parking lot, I saw the hearse parked

behind the building. I took a deep breath, laid my sunglasses aside, grabbed my notes, and stepped out of my car.

Inside, the funeral director greeted me and explained the family's wishes. They had decided not to walk in together at the start of the service. Instead, they preferred to find their seats naturally and spend a few moments mingling before it began.

That was fine with me. It meant I could find my seat and settle in before the service started. As I was getting mic'd up, I sensed someone standing next to me. I turned to see the pastor of the church waiting for me. She was a tall, slender woman dressed in a crisp power suit, and she got right to the point.

"Hello, Pastor Eaton. I'll show you where you need to be," she said.

"Okay, thank you," I replied.

She continued, "We have two different places for us to do ministry on our platform. The high place up there is only for me. Follow me to the only place you will be allowed to speak from."

CHAPTER 10 - RELATE CHANGES THINGS

Awkward, I thought to myself. But she wasn't done.

We walked to the platform. Hundreds of people had already gathered. She showed me where to sit and then where I was allowed to stand to deliver the message.

"Now, sit," she said, then turned and walked away.

I placed my things on my seat and followed her. "Where are you going?" she asked.

"I haven't seen the family yet. I want to say hi before we get started."

"No, I am going to be with the family. They're in the foyer, and I will be leading them into the service," she said. "You need to go sit down."

"I'm a little confused," I said. "The funeral director said the family didn't want a formal entrance. They just want to come in on their own."

"Oh no, they won't," she snapped. "I'm going to get them and lead them in. Now go sit down."

When the service began, the family had already seated themselves, just as they had planned.

Then I looked up and couldn't believe what I saw. Here came the pastor, somberly walking down the middle aisle—alone. No one followed her. It was surreal.

The family was heartbroken. They were hoping for some small comfort. The community had gathered to support them and remember a young girl.

This moment wasn't about the pastor—but she chose to make it about herself.

Thankfully, the service went well—a bittersweet time of sorrow mixed with celebration of this young girl's life. God's peace and hope were present.

The service concluded with me standing at the head of the casket, greeting everyone who wanted to pass by. After the last guests paid their respects, it was just the family and me. Through anguished tears, they took one last look at their beloved daughter, and we prayed together.

CHAPTER 10 - RELATE CHANGES THINGS

As is tradition, I stepped into the center aisle to lead the pallbearers carrying the casket out to the hearse.

Then, I felt someone touch my arm. I opened my eyes to see the funeral director, looking embarrassed.

"Reverend Eaton, I hate to ask this, but would you mind going to the back of the sanctuary so that the pastor of the church can lead the casket out?"

I looked to the back of the church, and there she stood, glaring at me.

"Absolutely, no problem," I replied. But I was lying. It was a problem. I thought to myself, This woman is crazy.

I moved to the back of the sanctuary and watched as the pastor proudly made a show of leading the casket out to the hearse. When it was over, I exited through a side door, still in disbelief.

While the funeral procession was being arranged, I sat in my car and opened my notes for the graveside service. A few minutes later, I looked up—and there she was, standing in front of my car, glaring at me again.

Without breaking eye contact, I slowly reached for my sunglasses and put them on.

Never in my life had I dreamed I would experience something like this—especially from another pastor!

It had been an incredibly tough week. I certainly didn't feel like I had "won" anything. No pastor wants to do a funeral for a child. I left that day shaken—but not angry.

RELATE helped me process the grief of this young girl's passing. It gave me the ability to do her funeral by naming why it affected me so deeply. My kids were around her age, and I couldn't imagine how devastating it would be to lose one of them. When I recognized my struggle was rooted in fear for my own kids' lives, I was able to bring it to God.

RELATE also helped me understand the host pastor's behavior. I saw how threatened she was by my presence.

Maybe she was wrestling with questions like, *Why wasn't I chosen to help?* or *What if this guy does a really good job, and*

CHAPTER 10 - RELATE CHANGES THINGS

my church realizes I'm not all they could have in a pastor?

Recognizing these possibilities allowed me to respond with compassion instead of offense. I could pray for her peace rather than holding onto resentment.

Even though her behavior was uncalled for, RELATE helped me not take it personally. I could let it go.

Simple Conflicts Remain Simple

My late wife, Angela, was deep into a project with the kids one day. She had been using RELATE for a few months. As dinnertime approached, I wanted to take some pressure off her, so I asked, "Do you want me to get something?"

"Yeah, that's fine. What are you thinking?" she replied.

Considering our budget and how we could feed all six of us easily, I said, "Papa Murphy's has their large double-stacked meat pizza for $15. How about that?"

If you've never seen this pizza, it's amazing! It's two pizzas in one, with a thick, rolled crust around the outside. It's so filling that just one pizza is enough for all of us.

"Fine," she replied.

I knew Angela well, and I knew that fine didn't mean good idea. It meant, go ahead and see what happens.

I asked, "What's wrong? Am I missing something?"

"No, I'm sorry," she said. After a few seconds of thought, she added, "I was threatened. I know you were just trying to help me. But I instantly felt like you weren't thinking of me and what I can eat."

I was blown away. She rerouted her thinking in real time!

That whole evening could have turned sour, but it didn't—because she recognized the story her brain was telling her wasn't true. She caught it, challenged it, and chose a different response.

All too often, simple conflicts turn into much bigger issues. How many divorces have been triggered by simple misunderstandings that could have been cleared up in seconds?

CHAPTER 10 - RELATE CHANGES THINGS

When you apply RELATE, it can change everything.

<< QUESTIONS TO REFLECT ON >>

- When you look back on recent conflicts or struggles in your relationships, can you identify how your own words or actions may have created a threat to someone else?

- In what ways have you seen small misunderstandings grow into major issues in your life? How might applying RELATE have changed the outcome?

- Do you tend to see yourself as the victim in relationship struggles, or do you take time to examine your role in the problem?

- Think about a time when someone else's insecurity or need for control created unnecessary tension. How could you have responded differently using RELATE?

- When have you experienced someone misusing their authority, like the pastor in this chapter? How can you practice compassion and peace rather than offense when you feel overlooked or disrespected?

- What is one simple conflict in your life right now that could be resolved by rerouting your thinking?

- How would your relationships change if you made it a daily habit to recognize and remove the threats you bring to others?

Conclusion

My grandfather knew the weight of extreme guilt firsthand. He spent years weighed down with regret. Early in his life he was involved in a car accident that was fatal for another driver. It was his negligence and life-choices that took a person's life. He spent some time in a workhouse to pay his debt to society, but it wasn't enough punishment to ease his conscience. After that he never drove again. The guilt stayed with him, and for years, he believed he was beyond redemption.

Even when my pastor visited him and shared the love and forgiveness of Jesus, he couldn't accept it. He didn't feel worthy of forgiveness. But the truth is, none of us are—that's the whole point of grace. Late in his life, my grandfather finally surrendered to Christ. Not because he deserved it, but because he realized that Jesus's blood was enough—even for him.

The Invitation: The God-Threat Removed

RELATE is God's way of doing relationships with us. He made a way to "just forgive." Jesus died on the cross for all sin, once and for all (1 Peter 3:18). Salvation is now about relationship—loving Him, knowing Him, respecting Him.

If there's anyone we should fear, it's God. Jesus made this clear when He said:

> *"Don't be afraid of people. They can kill you, but they cannot harm your soul. Instead, you should fear God who can destroy both your body and your soul in hell."*
> – Matthew 10:28 CEV

Jesus was showing us that the only real threat to our existence is God Himself. Solomon echoed this truth:

> *"The fear of the Lord is the beginning of knowledge."*
> – Proverbs 1:7 NIV

CONCLUSION

God wants you to understand that the greatest threat to your life is not knowing Him—not loving Him. Pride causes us to fear everything except God, but humility brings peace and hope.

> *"Humble yourselves, therefore, under God's mighty hand, that he may lift you up in due time. Cast all your anxiety on him because he cares for you."*
> – 1 Peter 5:6–7 NIV

Jesus modeled the RELATE process on the day He was crucified. From His prayer in the Garden to His final cry, *"It is finished!"* He rerouted His thinking. He elevated the Father and us. He listed His threats—extreme as they were. His life was being brutally taken. He was stripped and mocked publicly. His friends had abandoned Him. And yet, the cross was Jesus screaming to us: *Don't let them threaten you. Trust Me.*

But it was even bigger than that. On the cross, Jesus endured an agonizing death—beaten, mocked, humiliated—at the hands of His own creation. Why? Because He was making a statement. He was proving, in the most dramatic way possible, that He is not a threat to us. Through His suffering, God declared:

RELATE

Even though I am the only one you should fear, I am not here to destroy you—I am here to save you.

And now, the invitation is yours.

God doesn't want you on the wrong side of His story. He offers life, hope, and joy—even in the middle of life's struggles. He wants to redeem your past and turn even your worst moments into something meaningful. He wants to secure your eternity.

You're free to explore other religions in your search for security, status, and belonging—but none of them offer the promises of the living God. Jesus is the only One who conquered death. Every other so-called god is manmade.

You're also free to turn to substances to numb your fears. But when the high fades, the problems remain—often worse than before. You'll have lost time, money, and relationships. But here's the good news: when you've exhausted every other option, Jesus will still be waiting for you.

Or...you can surrender to Him now.

CONCLUSION

Jesus loves you. He has already paid the price for your sins. You are already forgiven. All He asks is that you trust Him.

There is no sin too big for the blood of Jesus. It's not about sin—it's about relationship.

Do you accept Him? Do you love Him? Will you surrender to what He loves and what He doesn't love, adjusting your life for Him?

Let God in. Trust Him. He stands at the door of your heart, waiting.

The invitation has your name on it. Accept it.

The Invitation: A Simple Prayer of Surrender

If you don't know how to pray, here are some words to help you:

God, thank you for your forgiveness. I understand you've invited me to know you. I believe you—help me with my unbelief. I want to know you, to know who you are, what you love, and what you don't love. Help me change my ways so I can make room for you to live inside me. In Jesus's name, Amen.

The Invitation: Living Above Your Threats

For those who are followers of Christ, shouldn't our lives look different from the world around us? What if every Christian took on the very attitude of Christ in their daily lives?

George Barna, a respected Christian sociologist and founder of the Barna Research Group, conducted extensive studies comparing the behaviors of Christians and non-Christians. His findings, shared in *The Second Coming of the Church*, revealed a sobering truth:

"We think and behave no differently from anyone else."

Barna's research showed little difference between Christians and non-Christians in key areas like divorce rates, financial habits, use of antidepressants, gambling, and overall life satisfaction. If we truly believe in the transforming power of Christ, shouldn't our lives reflect something different—something more?

CONCLUSION

What if we took God's way of thinking and living seriously? What if we embraced real, lasting change, change that didn't just adjust our personal habits but transformed the way we relate to others and the world? What if we lived above our threats?

Imagine the impact.

What if people could trust your integrity, your generosity, your wisdom—simply because you are a follower of Christ? What if you became the voice of calm and reason at work, the patient driver on the road, the neighbor who lifts others up?

This is the heart of RELATE. When we stop living in self-preservation mode and fully trust God, we're free to love others the way He calls us to. Change starts with two simple but powerful shifts:

- Managing the threats we face by surrendering them to God instead of trying to solve them through sin.

- Managing the ways we are a threat to others by becoming aware of how our actions impact those around us and intentionally choosing to bring peace instead of harm.

The Apostle Paul offered this charge to the early church—a message still relevant today:

> *"Now about your love for one another we do not need to write to you, for you yourselves have been taught by God to love each other. And in fact, you do love all of God's family throughout Macedonia. Yet we urge you, brothers and sisters, to do so more and more, and to make it your ambition to lead a quiet life: You should mind your own business and work with your hands, just as we told you, so that your daily life may win the respect of outsiders and so that you will not be dependent on anybody."*
> – 1 Thessalonians 4:9–12 NIV

Let's be different—not just in words, but in action. Let's live in a way that reflects Christ, a way that transforms us and the relationships around us.

CONCLUSION

<< QUESTIONS TO REFLECT ON >>

- In what areas of your life do your behaviors or attitudes look no different from the world around you?

- How would your relationships change if you fully embraced God's way of thinking and living?

- Where in your life do you need to stop living in self-preservation mode and start trusting God more?

- How do you typically respond when you feel threatened? How might surrendering those feelings to God bring peace to your relationships?

- In what ways might your actions, words, or attitudes pose a threat to others? How can you become more intentional about bringing peace and love instead?

- If someone observed your daily life, would they see the love of Christ reflected in how you treat others?

- What one step can you take today to start living differently—not just in words, but in action?

Sources

1. *Predisposed,* by John R. Hibbing, Kevin B. Smith, and John R. Alford

2. *Your Brain at Work,* by Dr. David Rock

www.ingramcontent.com/pod-product-compliance
Lightning Source LLC
Chambersburg PA
CBHW021146060526
44107CB00146B/1338/J